Contents

Open Your Mind
Before Your Business

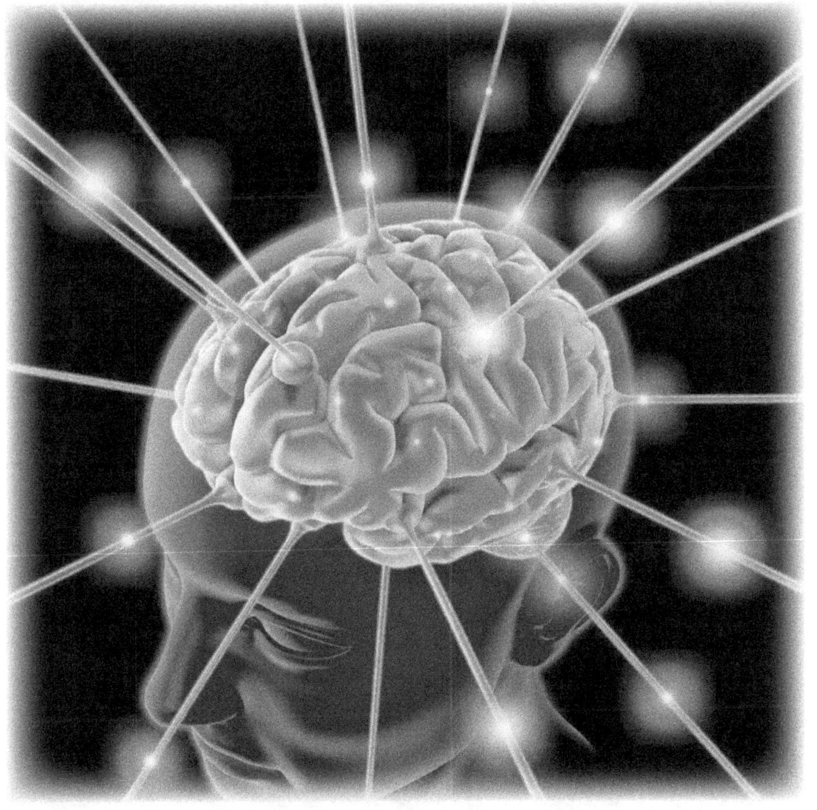

Empowering the Aspiring Entrepreneur

By Roland Troutman

Author's Bio

Roland E. Troutman Jr. was born October 16th, 1976 in Saginaw, Michigan to the parents of Bonnie Sledge and Roland E.Troutman Sr. Growing up as a child, my favorite subjects in school were English and math. I always dreamed of owning my own business. Besides being the father of two beautiful girls, I'm a professional sales person that made my bones in the auto industry as a top performer in the mid-Michigan area for over 10 years. I've sold new car lines such as; Cadillac, GMC, Chevrolet, Ford, Nissan and Hyundai. I've traveled the country helping dealers liquidate their used car inventory using refreshing techniques and a proven process.

In 2012, I decided to change industries and became a part of the business development of Internet Sales at Camping World of Fort Meyers, Florida. During my tenure there, I was the top sales performer consistently. I've used the extra money from sales to invest in small businesses and I've tasted sweet success. So as a way of giving back to the youth in all walks of life I decided to share my experiences…and write *Open Your Mind Before Your Business* to give the Aspiring Entrepreneurs a blue print, mentoring and guidance. I'm here to let everyone know when it comes to success, if you can dream it, you can achieve it.

Today, besides writing books, doing speaking engagements and seminars, I'm in the process of starting a franchise used car dealership.

Open your mind before your business
Empowering the Aspiring Entrepreneur

Written by: Roland Troutman
Art work by: Roland Troutman/ courtesy google free creation
logo artwork
Published by Trout House Publishing Company

ISBN 978-1-4951-7308-0

- 1 -
Who Am I?

Who am I? That simple question has never been easy for anyone to answer. Because it is who we are that defines how other people view our character, beliefs, strengths, and weaknesses. And with each interaction we have with different people, we also have varying personalities. Each person knows us in a different way, by degree of one or several of our multiple personalities. If someone would have asked me that question- *who am I?'*- In 1986, I would've said "Jordan", as I scoped up a left-handed layup to the basketball hoop. If you would've sat me down and asked me, in 1993 'who are you?' I would have responded with something along the lines of, "I'm a gangster, a thug."

The differences in my responses were largely attributed to my age and limited exposure to the environment in which I lived. In 1988, at the age of 12, I was full of vigor, dreams and hopes of a bright future amongst the stars. By age 16, things went terribly wrong; my uncle was addicted to crack, I was constantly fighting with my mother's boyfriend because he was a married man; it was also the year my father was murdered, shot in the head from a deal gone bad. As I think back it was my father's death, the way he died, that sent me on a road of destruction. By the age of eighteen, life set in and the realities that I experienced made me a different person. By 1999 I was in a desolate state of loneliness, depression and heart ache. My spirit had grown weary from a life of crime. We were drunk on superficial power and all too often I had put my faith in people, money and material things when I should've had my faith in God. I felt like I was suffocating in a fit of rage, I grew more paranoid with each passing day. I also knew that it was time to call it quits but I couldn't let the streets go and as such we did one final robbery. Little did we know that it was literally going to be our very last heist. We (my associates and I) decided to rob a bank in the heart of the city of Las Vegas on a sunny Saturday morning. Everything went wrong from the moment we started planning it and that should've been a sign to abort. But we didn't and I continued to ignore my conscious, which was pleading for me not to follow through with it. Nonetheless, we robbed the bank and I got caught. I ended up doing six years in a federal prison.

It took years for me to develop the volatile behavior that landed me in prison. So what happened? Where did I go wrong in life? Or even yet what went wrong in my life? Night after night, forced to examine my soul, I lay on my bunk bed staring at the ceiling too restless to fall asleep. I dreaded waking up looking at 2,000 other men. When I did manage to get sleep my dreams took me far away from my problems into a world of business and finance, and that's how the idea for this book was born.

As I did my time I built a wall of insecurity to protect my feelings from tragedy, abandonment, and heart ache mean-while, all along I was slowly dying inside. As I thought about my slow death, I realized that there was only one thing, or shall I say: One that could save me. I turned to Him and picked up my cross. My burdens were deep and heavy to bare but as I picked up my Bible and began to embrace the words of truth. I felt relieved, renewed. Over time the stress and pain began to subside and I no longer felt imprisoned, even though I was. Up until that moment, my life had been a peril of pain humming along to its own tune, a tune that played a rhythm of recklessness and lawlessness. I had felt as if life had failed me because that was the nature and design of the United States government as it related to their plan for black people (mainly black men) in this country-*total destruction*. But in reality the real enemy was myself, and other black males that were like me, with the same reckless and outlaw behavior- that slave mentality. We are responsible for at least a third of all murders of young black males that occur within our communities across the country, pick a city; Los Angeles, Detroit, Chicago, Saginaw, Vegas, Boston, Memphis, Miami. Get the point. We (black men) are public enemy # 1 for the lynching of other black men. This is nothing new, I'm not telling you something you don't already know. I'm merely re-enforcing a thought in hopes of change.

But why is it that (some) black people continue to blame the white race for their crime, degradation and poverty? The reason is simple to answer but very complex to solve, everyone needs a scapegoat, someone or something to blame when plans don't work out the way they were anticipated. As a result of many negative social issues such as low self-esteem, alcoholism, drug addiction, to the lack of parenting from the mother, father or both, and in most cases the lack of education by the parents, which then leads to minimum wage income and menial employment which is insufficient to provide for a family. All of these issues are contributors to why most (black people) blame the white race for their own shortcomings. But the question I pose is, do these accusations that are placed on the white race truly have any merit in regards to the successes or failures of this generation?

So who am I? I am a man that understands that racism still exists and I have accepted the fact that it will always exist, because all people need something or someone to hate. But I am also a man that has chosen the path of righteousness with the will to teach and make a positive difference in my life and other people lives that I come in contact with.

Let's fast forward to the present, and ask me that same question. Who are you? Today, I'm older with more responsibilities than 20 years ago, therefore my reply wouldn't be so curt and as such, my answer would require thought and reflection. Today, I would answer that question by saying that I am a man that has traveled a long road and endured a tremendous amount of pain and suffering. The pain and suffering that I endured was a combination of me not listening to my mother when I was growing up, watching my father brutally beat my mother, and feeling confused from growing up in a broken home without a positive male role model. Yes, I am a man with a troubled past that has the fortitude to achieve greatness. Although my story of hardship is probably no different than the average young black male growing up in inner city America, what is unique about mine is that I made it. I successfully beat the odds that were stacked against me, and so can you.

So who am I? I am a man that speaks from the heart and has compassion for my fellow human beings. I am a man with feelings of infinite love towards family and friends that

pledge eternal loyalty. I am a very confident man, secure with
who I am and I know exactly where I'm headed in life. I have
learned to live with the choices that I have made in my life and
I don't blame anyone but myself for the outcomes throughout
it. I have many contacts and friends in the United States and
abroad, where my name and reputation is diligent. Although I
don't have any gay friends to the best of my knowledge, I do
not discriminate, bash or hate them. I believe in the institution
of marriage and having one woman that I would love and trust
with my life. I am a father of a very intelligent and adorable
little girl and a wonderful step daughter in college; I love both
of them dearly. My ties within the community are solid, I've
sold cars and RV's for 10 years and made a decent living. I'm
currently a partner of a mid-size record label; I actively invest
in real estate among other investments and ventures in which I
will share with you later.

I no longer struggle with the pain of my father being
murdered years ago. I have accepted the fact that his life style
is what led to his untimely demise. And now it's time for me
to be a father, and as such, I shower my daughter with plenty
of hugs. I tell her how much I love her. I show her how much
I love her by spending most of my free time with her; we go
to the movies, skating, jogging or just to the park to hang
out. We shoot basketball, go beach bumming, sledding in the
winter, have water gun fights, reading and writing skills, out to
dinner dates and bar-b-cuing in the summer. I love her mother
and talk to her with kind words, not words of scorn and degradation.

We have plenty of good laughs and sometimes for the
hell of it, I cry simply because I needed a good cry to stay
sane. I'm not quite a ten. But I'm almost there based on my

connection and belief in the higher power, along with my faith and how I feel the relationship that I've established with God is. My spirit and belief is strong and will not falter. Change is inevitable and as such, I am thankful to God for the challenges in my life that I've had to overcome, as well as those times when others thought that I had failed. When in actuality, I was only getting better, getting stronger, learning more and perservering. But in order to understand what I'm saying, you have to experience and understand pleasure and grace, God's grace. And you must first feel pain with no mercy. If you don't get anything from this book, please remember; "In this world you have got to have nerves of titanium!" You must have the heart to achieve greatness! So please stay encouraged, stay energized, and never give up. But most of all stay humble and prayerful.

Earlier, I stated that 'I know where I am headed in life'. Do you know where you're headed in life? Where do you see yourself in ten years? What are your goals over the next five years? I also told you that I know who I am. Do you know who you are? Besides being whatever your first and last name is, the career you have and being the children of your parents, and the spouse of your wife or husband. We have to scratch below the surface to answer that question. We may have to expose some secrets and insecurities. I'm asking; do you really know who you are?

All of those dreams and hopes that you have of a bright future for your children, a nice spacious home for your family, the luxurious automobile, the cruises and vacations, the six figure bank account, impeccable credit. You have those desires because they are a part of who you are. If you just reach out, build a foundation and continue to fight, you can live those dreams. They will become your reality. Well I'm going to tell you how you can find out who you are; we're going to build a foundation of ***physical, psychological, spiritual, and financial strength.*** So ask yourself, 'who am I and where am I going? Be honest with yourself. Don't be afraid to admit that you are in a bad situation and need some help. Then you will know how important it is to set goals, formulate a strategic plan, and execute each step as if your life depended upon it. And by the end of this book you should be able to evaluate yourself and have an answer to the aforementioned questions.

- 2 -
Where Are You Going?

Life has a strange way of bringing you to the person that you are meant to be in life. The road that we travel is determined by our will power. Our will is what makes us want to be independent and consciously free with a purpose or meaning in life far beyond mediocrity. Remember; the decisions that we make influence our actions. Consequently it is our actions that corrupt our souls. So where are you going in your life? What are you doing to constructively impact your life or someone else's in a positive, productive way? Do you give charity with humility and good intentions, or are you motivated by motive? Let's examine what it means to be motivated by motive. Well, according to the American Heritage dictionary the word motivate is defined as: to provide with an incentive to move into action, impel. And the word motive means an emotion, desire, need or similar impulse that causes a person to act. Being motivated by motive means you allow greed, money, or profits or some form of gain to dictate your actions in life. Some consider this type of personality shrewd. In reality this type of person is very superficial. Money or greed should never be your reason for doing something. Your motive should always be to help others.

For example if you find a way to benefit others you will always be successful in all that you set out to do. For charity is the path to the heart of God. And God takes care of those who take care of His children. Life is special and so are you because God gave you life. So live to love and love because it's right.

I present several questions that I challenge you to honestly answer because it is crucial to a true evaluation of yourself. Do you set goals? What are your personal values, your principles? What do you stand for? Do you feel that your life has any significance or real meaning in this world? Do you believe in or support a positive peaceful cause that can make a difference in your neighborhood, your city, your state, your country or even save a life? Do you exercise? Have you given any thought to your health? Let's discuss our health. I too am slacking in this department. Although I am aware of the healthier food choices, I don't always eat what's best nor do I exercise as often as I should-no excuses.

So, in order to build wealth we must first be in tune with the Creator, submit to His will and become a faithful child of God. So therefore we have to take care of our body with the proper diet and exercise. After all, what good is wealth if you don't have good health to enjoy it? Good health starts in the mind. It is sparked by a thought and a fear at the same time. The fear of growing old and weary lingers subliminally in the back of all of our minds. But it is the thought of living longer; looking better or sexier for our mates or potential mates, feeling good and being physically fit and strong that propel us most. However, positive thinking is only a small key to building good health. Positive actions coupled with positive re-enforcement are very vital to sustaining your health. Most people are not aware of the dangers of cardiovascular disease, diabetes, and high blood pressure. These are all silent killers that are preventable if we apply ourselves to a few simple, yet positive routines.

Let's talk about cardiovascular or "heart disease" and discuss some of the risk factors associated with it. Cardiovascular disease is the number one killer of both men and women in the United States and globally. Coronary heart disease is the most common type of heart disease, killing more than 370,000 people annually. This condition occurs in the arteries that are responsible for the movement of blood to and from the heart, that now have become hard and narrow due to an excessive buildup of plaque. Heart attack and stroke occur when this blood flow has stopped. There are several preventable risk factors that contribute to heart disease. They include: high blood pressure; smoking; high LDL cholesterol; diabetes; obesity; physical inactivity; poor diet and excessive alcohol use.

High blood pressure–which is also known as hypertension is also a part of cardiovascular disease. Hypertension can destroy our bodies because it makes the heart work harder and it may cause the heart to enlarge. If your heart enlarges too much and it can no longer meet the demands of your body then you can possibly suffer from elevated blood pressure levels-also known as hypertension. But there are other variables as well, which we shall discuss. There are some very important risk factors that are associated to cardiovascular disease that we can control.

Cigarettes and tobacco smoke are the most prevalent risk factors because smoking decreases good cholesterol levels or HDL (high density lipoprotein) and according to recent medical studies, high levels of HDL greatly reduces your chance of a heart attack because it carries cholesterol away from your heart.

Low density lipoprotein (LDL) is also referred to as bad cholesterol and too much of this can clog your arteries and therefore increasing your chances of a heart attack and/or stroke. Furthermore, besides hardening of the arteries, in time because the arteries have hardened from smoking, it can stop or prevent an erection in men because nicotine constricts blood vessels and slows down blood flow whenever it's in our bodies. So stop now if you want to live longer!

Low Fitness levels are also related to cardiovascular diseases. Research has shown that people who exercise throughout their life even engaging in cardio-fitness are more likely to live a longer and healthier life than those who do not. So now is the time to start walking, power-walking, light jogging, stretching, and getting in shape. Take your time, start slow and gradually build up to more intense exercises such as weight lifting, aerobics, yoga, or kick boxing. Your mental capacity also plays a very vital role in determining your over-all physical health. Such as one lifts weights and eats the proper foods so that the physical muscles may grow. The same holds true for the brain, which is also a muscle in its own class. It needs proper nourishment, exercise, and knowledge of a positive substance in order to grow. If the brain is stimulated in a negative manner then what you will see is the devolving and subtle mental deterioration of a person. In time you'll find exercising to be not only a great stress reliever but fun and reinventing both spiritually and mentally.

Poor Eating Habits or improper dieting is the single most risk factor that we can control. We can reduce the chances of diabetes, high cholesterol, high blood pressure, and heart attack by simply changing our eating habits to a healthy diet. Healthy foods lead to a healthier sound mind and body.

There is great harm done to the human body being a meat eater. Beef is very dangerous for you because it takes 3 days to fully digest. It also contains parasites requiring the meat to be cooked to at least 150 degrees Fahrenheit to kill them. Beef also contains growth hormones that are being injected into the cows to fatten them up quicker. These growth hormones contain different chemicals such as bovine, that scientist have shown are parallel to cancer. Beef is also loaded with saturated fats and cholesterol which is the primary cause of heart disease and high blood pressure.

Pork also takes at least 3 days to completely digest. However, pork contains over 19 different worms such as; the ring worm, round worm, flat worm, tape worm, trichina worm just to name a few. Pork must be cooked to at least 165 degrees Fahrenheit to kill most of these parasites.   Both of these meats cause our bodies to bloat, gain excess fat and make us appear swollen due to its slow digestion process and harmful chemicals. So we should all strive from this day forward to rid ourselves of meat and its harmful effects, which takes years off of our lives. A diet of grains such as rice's and cereals, poultry; such as eggs or baked chicken, fruits, vegetables and if you must eat meat, fish is a good replacement. Fish is loaded with protein which is good for muscle growth and sustaining energy.

Now that we have an idea of how to take care of our body lets discuss the process of building our minds. Our minds are the key to unleashing our will to win. A strong mental capacity will decimate any opponent. You must learn to see every situation as many variables, similar to the game of chess when thinking two or three moves ahead of your opponent.

Let's think of our glasses as being almost full instead of half empty. Optimism has never been for the weak, it was designed to give the strong an even greater leverage. Your time to shine has come. But you must remain patient, focused, and diligent. By all resolve continue to strive with intelligence. Stay motivated and I wish you all good health!

- 3 -
History of Social Order

We must first know what has happened and where it happened in order to understand what we need to do and where we want to go in life. Drawing upon the history and evolution of people and how civilizations came to be, I and other sociologist identify with five types of societies. The first society is hunting and gathering society, which meant the men, hunted the large animals and the women would hunt for the smaller ones. The entire society was expected to work by either hunting or picking/gathering berries, nuts, and various vegetation. As a result of gathering and hunting the food supply in one area dwindles and then the society made up of around 30 to 40 people would simply pick up and move on. This caused the society to become nomadic.

The revolution of domestication ushered in a new society of horticultural and pastoral society as people both hunted animals and planted their foods, this society lived very close to the water, they were not nomadic. The concept of pastoral came about because people discovered that they could tame some of the animals that they hunted and as a result a different society was created, simultaneously people were discovering that they could influence the cultivation of a plant and as a result people began to use hand-made tools to cultivate their plants, this was the first type of farming.

However the domestication of animals and cultivating of plants changed society because groups or societies grew bigger due to the enormous supply of food. As a result of such a vast amount of food, less and less people were required to help with providing food so people began to branch out and make other things such as tools, jewelry, clothing, weapons and even slaves of black people. This brought about trade and war among each other and ushered humans into the 2nd social revolution, the agricultural society.

The agricultural society came about because one special tool was invented, the plow. Using an animal to plow the soil they dug up more of the earth's nutrients which made food more abundant. This allowed people to occupy their time doing other things such as art, language; music and sex. And as a result small societies grew into developed into cities. But as the wheel and numbers were also created within this great social boom, so was inequality and social class, those who controlled the growing of food and had more control of their crops made more money and levied taxes on those with less power thus bringing about an imbalance of social class and power while taking us into the Industrial Revolution.

The industrial society between 1765 and the 1900's was the biggest change and also yet the time where the most social inequality took place. Technology changed society forever. The steam engine was now running machinery, work conditions were horrible and unsafe, there weren't any labor laws, going on strike was illegal, and the ancestors of former slaves were denied the right to vote and were treated less than uncivil, the same held true for all women as well, they had no rights.

Those workers that chose to strike were shot by police or the National Guard. But as time progressed us into the 1960's things were heated as riots and protests gave way to somewhat relevant treatment to some people but not equal treatment of all people. Segregation and civil rights were a major battle ground as the Jim Crow laws were slowly done away with; women began to get some rights as well. This brings us into the Post Industrial Society also known as the Information Societies or the information age and this is our 4th social revolution and changing into our fifth type of society.

In the information society, people provide services rather than produce goods. People are no longer holding onto past traditions and family values. Information is our main asset and tool for earning money. The major invention of this society was the microchip. This society is extremely technology driven. With the inventions of email, text messaging, smart phones, androids, sync- pads, the iPod, laptops, notebooks, MySpace, Facebook, Twitter, and Google, our world has gotten smaller while our power to create and connect has expanded. Feminism has emerged, which is good because that gives way to equal rights for everyone.

Throughout society the different gender roles changed as women fought for their rights and as society progressed to the point that there were an abundance of food and wealth. In the information society, women are independent and much more empowered and have made tremendous contributions to the sectors of business and music, for example Sheryl Sandberg – who at one point in time happened to be 2nd in command at Facebook, serving as COO. Previously, Sandberg worked as Vice President of Operations for Google as well. She also served as Chief of staff for the United States

Treasury Department. Women have also been very influential in education, look at Maya Angelou, politics-Hilary Clinton just to name a few. While we are on the subject of empowering women I'd like to share with you a brief history of the struggles that women have endured at the hands of men. This is a story that I'd written in college about a lady name Mary Wollstonecraft. As you read along I want you to try to imagine how hard and difficult of a time Mary must've had back then. But it was her core character that kept her pushing forward with her agenda.

Life and Times of a Fighter

The story, "On National Education", is a very heartfelt and courageous work. The author Mary Wollstonecraft does a phenomenal job tackling the issues of sexism against women, equal education in both the public and private schools for girls and boys, the institution of marriage and women empowerment. Mary was a British writer that lived during a time of the French Revolution. She was considered to be a radical and a liberal of her time because of her thoughts, beliefs, and ideology on equal rights for women. Throughout the entire writing Mary not only identified the moral and social degradations that women faced but she also offered solutions to the significance of women being properly and equally educated. Such as if women were to be properly educated they would ultimately become better wives and as such the wives would be motivated to do their domestic duties even better than before. Mary Wollstonecraft made the connection between education and self-esteem by explaining that if properly educated women would then be ashamed of their crafty ways and no longer indulge themselves in such deviance. Furthermore education would help do away with most women's manipulative actions, and subservient attitudes, in which case women would no longer busy their days doing simple, practical things that had no meaning. She believed that marriage would never be held sacred or of any value until men began to respect the sacred vows and treat women as their companion and equal. Mary was an advocate for the rights of women politically, socially, and economically by addressing the oppression of women through her writings and redefining the role of women by her actions to make her point. Mary was speaking to men, but mainly to men in power as she challenged them to treat their wives with more respect and allow women to become better by leveling the social classes and making proper education accessible to everyone. Her purpose of this writing was to open society's eyes and bring attention to the injustices and cruel treatment that women were subjected to.

Mary challenged the institution of marriage by painting a picture of bleakness for both men and women using the appeal of emotions effectively as she says, "marriage is the cement of society, mankind should all be educated after the same model, or the intercourse of the sexes will never deserve the name of fellowship, nor will women ever fulfill the peculiar duties of their sex, till they become enlightened citizens, till they become free by being enabled to earn their own subsistence, inde-pendent of men." (Wollstonecraft 36). She went on to further mitigate her point that women will never see marriage as holy and matrimonial as men because of the woman's low self-es-teem as a result of being treated undignified by their husbands. "Nay marriage will never be held sacred till women, by being brought up with men, are prepared to be their companion rather than their mistress." (Wollstonecraft 36). Mary's intentions were very clear as she successfully made her point by the direct force as she presented methods in which to give women hope and empowerment while helping men see that life would be much better for them if women had a higher self-esteem.

Mary's use of appeal and the occasional flirt with anecdote was effective in addressing the cultural factors of her time that women were forced to tolerate. Her use of anecdote was strong and emphatic upon how women degraded themselves with their insecure mindset. She pointed out how women did silly things because of their lack of independence. Mary also brought up the nature of women, which had true understanding, not lacking knowledge, she would, "have the privilege of conveying pure joy to the heart." (Wollstonecraft 37). She offered a unique perspective drawing upon her own observations of women doing cunning and sly maneuvers to get what they want their male over-seer, as she used the analogy, "I have been desired to observe the pretty tricks of a lapdog that my perverse fate has forced me to travel with." (Wollstonecraft 37). Mary compared the silly tricks and shallow ways of women to the behavior of a dog. She further explained how boys grew into men and as such they also changed in behavior and treatment toward women, but the behavior was learned early in school, as she said, "the transition as they grow up from barbarity to brutes to domestic tyranny over wives, children, and servants, is very easy." (Wollstonecraft 42).

Mary was once again comparing humans to animals. Although she used pathos, seething anger to get her point across logos is present she described the way and why boys grow to become abusive husbands and fathers. The strategies that Mary used along with the examples aforementioned are effective in reaching her audience while simultaneously proving that women are inferior to men. The analogies used gave power to her writing by showing how men and women should be treated equally. Mary painted a very vivid description to bring to light the inequalities of women. Her examples sparked the emotion of women and the problems they were facing.

Mary Wollstonecraft bravely took a stance to give voice to women, relying heavily on the emotions of pathos. She used diction and tone while speaking boldly to men about their innate fear of allowing women to flourish. She rejected the deep -rooted insecurity that has plagued the male gender since the beginning of time by saying, "to render mankind more virtuous and happier of course, both sexes must act from the same principles; but how can that be expected when only one is allowed to see the reasonableness of it?" (Wollstonecraft 43). The appeal she created was pathos, as if feeling slighted or bitter towards the unreasonableness of men or their lack of comprehension to such as simple and plain but beautiful solution to everyone's happiness. Mary further proved her point by stating that in order for us all to be equal we must all be free and receive the same schooling that the aristocrats and men received. She made the assertion that if you have a good husband and father then you will have a good wife and mother when she said, "make women rational creatures, and free citizens and they will quickly become good wives and mothers; that is if men do not neglect their duties as husbands and fathers." (Wollstonecraft 44).

The writing "On National Education" by Mary Wollstone-craft redefined a genre. It is as radical as it is empowering and encouraging for all people. It was a challenge to men in power to level the social classes, treat women with compassion and decency, and usher in co-ed schooling along with equal education. This writing was the first of its kind to take such a liberal approach by a female author. It reached its target audience predominantly through the logos and pathos appeal while intertwining common sense analogies to real life situations. Although she made generalizations based upon her own observations of how women behaved around or towards their husbands she also referenced the need for equal education to create a more free society which would ultimately better the lives of families.

Social Status Verses Social Roles

The social status and social roles of a person are dramatically different from one another. A social status is a person's standing or class within their society. This status is usually based on some form of prestige or the lack thereof. It's usually power driven. For Instance a person wants to own a Rolls Royce simply because they can. That person could've bought any car, like every other common *Joe*. However, the common Joe can't afford to buy the Rolls Royce. So the Rolls Royce gives that person a perception of status, prestige, being a few notches above everyone else. Whereas a social role is how you behave, it is your style or "swag" as the youngsters are saying now. It is how your society has helped to define who and what you are. It is how you are viewed by yourself and society. For example my social role in society is a real estate investor, car salesman and father. However my status is middle class. The difference between role conflict and role strain is when things that are expected of us while we are in one role- actually collides or goes against with what is expected of us from our other roles. For example sometimes what my role is as a son actually is totally disagreeable with my role as a mate to my special lady. My mom wanted me to go to church with her at

8 o'clock in the morning and that special lady want me to stay
at home for some housecleaning. Neither of them knew about
the other wanting my time. But because of my different roles,
with two different people, it brought about a social conflict.

<u>So the question I pose is:</u>
<u>Can the size of a group affect the overall function of the group?</u>

In my opinion, yes the size of a group can affect the overall
function; for example as the societies grew and we moved into
the industrial revolution the role of the women and children
changed. Women and children no longer had to gather food or
hunt. Women became the home caretaker and children were
then shuttled off to school to get an education. Also the bigger
the group only adds to responsibility that creates different jobs
and things people can do to make a living. Sometimes the size
of a group can affect how a presidential election or vote goes.
If a person is against a certain issue they might not be so quick
to speak up because the majority of the group is for a certain
issue.

I think it is unique that sociologist and people in general
view deviance purely as a means of survival. Whereas, if they
don't view it as an action but it is merely a deviation or change
or switch from the norm, then deviance is the direct violation
of norms. It's the reaction from our society that makes the
behavior deviant, based on what society deems to be appro-
priate. For example the United States views polygamy as
deviant. But in other countries and certain religions polygamy
is viewed as being normal, as a way of life. Another example
is how money and business guru's like Donald trump and
others making business deals to profit millions and then they
write books or talk about their exploits. In China, up until just

recently, that was a crime punishable by death and it was called profiteering. China considered such bravado to be taboo or deviant.

In the film People like Us: Social Class in America there were several different social concepts. One social concept that I found interesting was that middle class blacks chose to call themselves "black middle class" as if because of their race they were considered not to be the norm for middle class. The question I posed to myself was why couldn't they just simply consider themselves "middle class" and omit race, creed, and ethnicity from the equation. If they were in the middle class income bracket of earning at least 60,000 dollars per year, which is equivalent to other families and singles earning the same income in the United States, then why did they feel the need to distinguish themselves from the rest of the middle class Americans?

Let's discuss in detail how this is relevant to the current topics of Social Class in the United States, Social Stratification, and Race and Ethnicity because all of these topics create a certain mindset, a bold and deliberate way of thinking. Each mindset creates a different concept of life, which in turn, create the environment in which a person of a particular class or group live within. The environment, in which we live, more often than not, dictates our choices and actions in our everyday life. Our character, personality, morals, values, and even our children are all affected by our environment and life style choices. Our social class is defined by how we believe other people perceive us. The film People like Us: Social Class in America said that "in America it is not always about race but about class." But it's the choices that you make that reveal your social class. Having money enables a person or family to create whatever lifestyle desired as long as that lifestyle is accepted by your social class.

Now let us examine Social Stratification. Social stratification is a system in which groups of people are divided into layers according to their relative property, power and prestige (Essentials of Sociology, 162). Every society in the world is divided into groups. Groups and division is how basis's come about. There are many different forms of division such as sexism, the practice of prejudice and discrimination of someone because of their gender. There's racism, the practice of prejudice and discrimination towards someone because of their race or skin color. Each division creates its own society, its very own social stratification. As such the social stratification also divides people based upon the amount in their bank account, the type of car a person drives, the type of clothes worn, jewelry, reputation, status and political influence a person possesses.

So if a person or family earning 60,000 dollars per year is considered to be middle class, which is their social class and following the definition of social stratification, then why would a race of people that fit within the aforementioned social class choose to separate themselves from their social class by form of stigma based on their race and ethnicity? Is it because of how that particular race feels that this is how their society regards them? Or is their own insecurity merely acting out to the known stereotypes filtered throughout the pulverized black communities? In my opinion the "middle class blacks" felt that they didn't fit into the class of most of their black family and friends because they weren't poor anymore but they also felt that they were still black and regardless of their achieved success and education, they just didn't fit in with most middle class Americans either, whom happened to be white. So they formed their own stratification and their own community and the concept became "black middle class." I'm not suggesting that separating themselves is neither good nor bad, it's their preference. But at the end of the day when the sun sets, I know one thing for sure, there's only one flag flying over all of our heads. We're all Americans right down to the core of our souls; white, black, red, yellow and brown.

Karl Marx believed that society was made up of two social classes; the capitalist that owned everything and the exploited worker. He believed that there should be a balance and that the exploited workers should unite and untie those horrendous straps of injustice and fight back. He was kicked out of Germany for his rebellious ideology.

There are multiple reasons why the middle class is shrinking. First let's examine the number of qualified individuals in the United States that have the necessary credentials that employers require. With the ever changing fast pace of our world, the ever increasing need, use, and creation of technology, along with the depletion of unskilled blue collar jobs such as General Motors a ripple effect has been created causing incomes to diminish and as a result both families and individuals have moved to a lower social class. As of this writing, unemployment is still well above 9 percent nationally and as high as 10 percent in Michigan. Also as taxes, gasoline and oil prices continue to rise, the real estate market is stagnant and our stock market is volatile. These things also play a major role in why the middle class is shrinking and so are our human rights.

Human rights are principles, guaranteed through the process of natural order, that are fundamentally regarded as being free from unlawful imprisonment, torture, execution, bodily harm, and freedom of expression without persecution as long as those persons exercising those rights do so without violating the human rights of their fellow human. My idea of universal human rights are: for everyone to Respect one another, Charity to those less fortunate- if we all truly played our part there would be no more hunger or homeless people. Cherish women and treat them with grace and tenderness because they bear our future. Love and educate our children and prepare them to become entrepreneurs, leaders, nurturing parents and loving spouses'.

In order to fully explain and understand the social imagination of almost anyone and its importance to the study of sociology, we must first look at what sociology is. Sociology is the study of different cultures and communities and how we (people) react within our environment. But it's also deeper than that, sociology also deals with the consequences and rewards from our actions and reactions. So that means that the sociological imagination is our society or community's way of thinking. But it is also our independent thought process or way of viewing the world, our life and people around us. The sociological imagination influences everything and everyone around us. It is so powerful that our languages, clothing, foods, and feelings even our mates, lovers and life partners are all influenced by the very fabric of the sociological perspective.

The importance of the sociological perspective is expressed in the United States for example; when we are in public and most people know that there are certain things you don't do such as men exposing their private parts or women walking around topless. These are things from our country's sociological perspective to be indecent. My point is that the sociological

perspective provides both written and unwritten boundaries
for the purpose of maintaining civility, human interaction and
survival.

The four key components of sociology are; the systematic
study which deals with the influences, the culture, their beliefs
and general practices.

1. The systemic component deals with how and the way
    things work in an environment and why they work that
    way?
2. The second component is the individual. This pertains
    to the thoughts, feelings, and actions of people based
    upon our need as humans to express our emotions and
    act out our thoughts. Think of it as a freedom that could
    never be set free. Otherwise there would be total chaos
    due to the variance of personalities and opinions of all
    the humans on the planet.
3. Social Institutions such as banks, credit unions, political
    offices, the news and media, face book, twitter, Google,
    the stock market, the military, homeless shelters, prisons,
    and even retail stores are all prime examples of social
    institutions that have influenced, shaped, defined or rede-
    fined who we are. It is necessary because that is how we
    evolve and continue expanding upon our knowledge and
    development but more importantly, technology is ever
    so crucial to advancement of human survival. But do we
    depend on our technology too much?
4. Religion is the fourth component of sociology. Religion
    is the belief in a deity or higher power who someone
    believes is responsible for our successes or failures
    in life. Religion allows us to tap into our conscience

and discern right from wrong. I feel we are prisoners
of our socialization based on the different personalities, religions and behaviors of each individual. It is a
blessing that we get along this well. I understand that
we all must put our core family values, personal and
racial feelings to the side and try to understand how one
another live. But even the willing participants know
that integration is painful. But it is their fortitude that
will continue to usher in change and positive growth.
I don't believe that racism is so much a "cultural practice" as oppose to being what I call "universal insanity".
Universal insanity is the repetition of doing something over and over- even if it is harmful or potentially
fatal- until you no longer expect different results, for
you have merely accepted the negative behavior's and
therefore you have incorporated it into your life style.

Many scientists believe that race doesn't exist in the natural
world but does exist in the social world. The "natural" world
is considered to be the 'the world of science'-DNA. According
to scientific studies, all human beings are 99.99 percent genetically the same therefore eliminating race as a factor. We all
have a chemical in our bodies called Melanin. The word
Melanin is derived from the Greek word melanos, which means
black. Melanin is considered by scientist to be the *giver of
life'* because depending on how much melanin a person has
in their body will determine eye color, hair color and most of
all outer layer skin pigmentation. Those with a high content of
melanin will most likely have a darker hue to their skin-tone,
while those with lesser amount of melanin will probably have a
lighter skin complexion. But melanin or the lack thereof is one

of many variables in science while unlocking the truths that race does exist. Another 'natural world' variable is geographical location working in conjunction with genetic mutation. In other words where people reside not only affects their social order, determine their lifestyle but our bodies in time and over time will adapt and adjust to the climate of the region we reside in. For example; the closer people are to the equator, such as people born and raised in Cuba or Brazil, are highly probable to have a darker skin complexion and a different hair texture than a person that was born and raised in Prague. The reason for this is because our outer layer of skin is a protective layer and our first line of defense from germs and anything the body deems unsafe so therefore our body and skin adapts and adjust according to nature for the sole purpose of our survival.

However, in the social world our eyes have been trained to only see the physical. The physical view of a group of people gives distinction, classification and grouping. Race is the concept of how groups separate themselves from other groups. Race is a reality, we are all different. Race does exist and everyone should stop denying it. Race cannot be deter- mined by blood type but rather we as people stigmatize and classify ourselves. I have taken the time to research the word Aryan and the history of Aryanism. What I found was quite intriguing.

The word Aryanism comes from the root word Arius. Arius was a man that lived during the Roman emperor Constantine, from 256 to 336 A.d. He was a theologian that was born in Libya. Arius's doctrine was that God created Christ, and therefore Arius believed that Christ was less than God, but higher in creation than man. After Arius's death his doctrine became known as Aryanism and was embraced by the masses of Greece and Rome.

However by 325 A.d. the doctrine was suppressed and banned from practice within the empire. Although it did survive in its purest forms amongst the barbarians- they had no power to keep it alive or in the mainstream. By 496 A.d. the teaching's became distorted and used as a platform of hate and separatism for those of an insecure mindset seeking separatism. So I say that the Aryanism that is being practiced and taught today is a far cry from the teaching's that Arius had intended to be given to the people. The Aryanism of today is of an imposter doctrine. The only color that matter in this world now is green, and the only race that matter; is the race to the finish line of business and politics.

In the social world it is the dominant group- also recognized as the majority that does the discriminating upon the minority group. The unfair or unequal treatment is done by controlling the political power, wealth, and the sharing of similar physical and cultural characteristics. The dominant group actually creates race as a means to single out or inflict unfair treatment towards the minority group. The aforementioned of dominant control is by design and the very reason why it has withstood throughout time.

Let's compare and contrast the terms stereotype, prejudice and discrimination. The definition of stereotype is an idea that many people have about a thing or group that may often be untrue or partly true. An example of a stereotype is that all Black people can dance or all Mexican people speak Spanish, which both statements are simply not true. Because not all black people can dance, I'm living proof of that and nor does every Mexican speak Spanish. Prejudice is very different from a stereotype, whereas prejudice is defined as prejudging a group or thing as inferior and usually in a negative manner.

An example of prejudice would be; for a Caucasian father to tell his son 'not to like black people because their looks are different than us.' Finally let's take a look at discrimination. Discrimination is an action of unfair treatment directed against someone. Discrimination can come in many forms based on age, weight, height, skin complexion, clothing, education, marital status, gender and sexual preference. For instance if someone wanted to look at a house and I told them that I will only show the home to white people or only to tall people, that would be a form of discrimination. Stereotype, prejudice and discrimination intermingle because the stereotype which is usually exploited by the media or dominant group gives way to the social prejudice and as a result of the social prejudice; discrimination is then perpetrated by the dominant group.

Using my sociological imagination I believe that there are strong commonalities between race and gender. Both race and gender have their own communities or groups and therefore can at times be a dominant group or a minority. Both race and gender can either do the discriminating or either be discriminated against. Race and gender are descriptive words used to define the physicality of what someone or something is. For example a man is a gender and he can show prejudice and discrimination towards a person of a different gender such as a woman or a transgendered person.

Life is a struggle for justice and most people are faced with the challenge of rising beyond the realms of a poverty stricken economic stature. Still, others deny themselves the opportunity to rise in the corporate world or in life over-all because of poor appearance, lack of quality education, unwillingness to listen to instructions and directions, afraid to attempt to achieve success against all odds, laziness and self-pity. However, skin racism still exists subconsciously in the minds of those who have the controlling power of information, wealth, and the media. This example of racism and prejudice exists on an artificial level in the minds of the weak, scared and / or modern day hate mongers also known as extremists', militia radicals.

- 5 -
What is Wealth?

Before we can become wealthy, we must first know what wealth is and how to obtain it? But in order to obtain it, we must first know where it is and who has it? Wealth is defined by Webster's dictionary as an abundance of possessions or resources. Affluence, riches. The way in which wealth is obtained is by either generating from a pre-existing financial pipeline or creating a stream line of huge ROI (return on investments), while contributing very little labor. So let's explore where the wealth is and find out who has it. We are also going to cover how you can get your slice of the pie and live a comfortable and plentiful lifestyle. Throughout this chapter I want you to remember that poverty is a very harsh and cruel reality in life and it is felt throughout the world. Poverty creates homelessness and much social sadness. However, being poor or broke is a temporary mind state, a psychological illness that can be corrected.

So who has all the wealth? And how can you obtain your share? The people that have the wealth are divided into financial classes and you must cross each financial class or threshold to finally make it to the top 2% elite Ultra-rich. It has been known for quite some time that the top 5% wealthiest people in the United States either own or control nearly 93% of the country's wealth. There is a very small percentage of Americans that have a net worth ranging from 1.1 billion to 66 billion, placing them in the social class- *Ultra Rich, a very exclusive club.* According to a report by UN University, 2% of the nation's population own or control 98% of the nation's

Financial Social Classes

Social Class	Income Generation	U.S. %
Poor	$5k to 25,000 per yr.	64%
Middle class	26,000 to $74,000 per yr.	18%
Affluent (upper middle class)	75,000 to 99,000 per yr.	10%
Rich	100,000 to1 million per yr.	6%
Ultra-Rich	1 million or More per month	2%

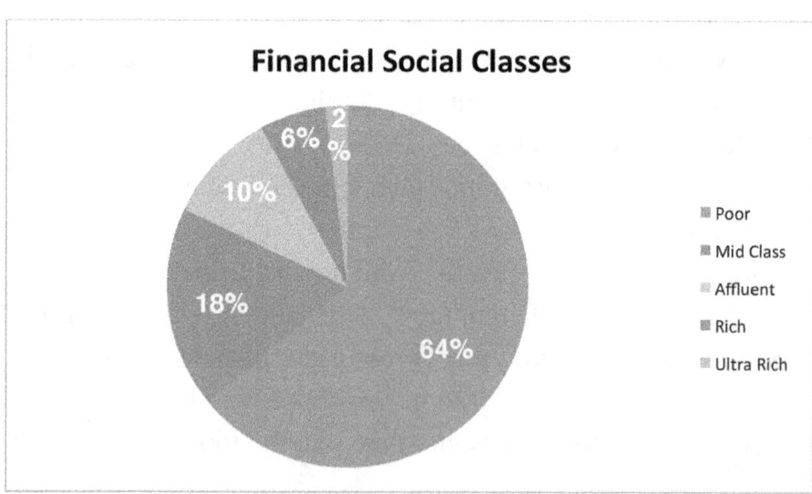

wealth. This roughly equates to the lifestyle and resources obtained by ultra-rich billionaires generating supreme earning power. Though it's true that a millionaire is born every day, the same doesn't hold true for billionaire's. Above is a breakdown of financial social classes and which percent of the population of the U.S. fit into each category.

The previous pie chart is what the United States Economic- Social Structure looks like. The 64% represent the people struggling to make it every day, they are poor. While the ultra-rich represent the 2% controlling the strings of the land. Now that you know what wealth is and who has it. It's time to discuss how to get your share of the pie.

There are many things that a person could do to earn money but what good is earning the money if you don't know how to keep and expand your wealth? So the first thing a person should do is figure out what they would like to do and write a business plan or a planned budget- how much you have to invest in your own business. Then assemble a dream team around that plan. A dream team is your team of professionals that work for you. Such as your banker, real estate broker, several attorney's; (tax attorney, real estate, corporate attorney), Insurance broker, accountants, auditor, stock trader. Remember successful people create and structure highly successful teams!!

Below is a list of Idea's for a business:
Best all-around business:
- Cleaning Service
- Consultant of all type
- Medical transcription Service
- Repair Service- (all types)

Business easiest to start:
- Cleaning service
- Errand service
- In-home Healthcare
- Pet sitting service/ Pet grooming service
- Grow Specialty foods/ Products Shop
- Travel Sales Agency

Businesses w/ Highest Earning Potential:
- Professional Consultant (all types)
- Employee Executive Recruiter/ Training Staff
- Business Broker
- Bill Auditing service
- Internet Information Technologies Firm

Low Startup Cost Businesses:
- Bookkeeping Service
- Family child care provider
- In Home Healthcare
- Private Investigator
- Professional Planner
- Technical Writer
- Transcriptionist
- Makeup Artist

Fastest-Growing Occupations:
- Cleaning Services
- Computer Techs
- Medical Transcriptionist
- I.T. Tech
- Fitness Trainer
- Home Restoration Service
- Caterer
- Computer Programmer

- Moving Service
- Mortgage Broker
- Realtor
- Loan officer/ Agency
- Start your own secured credit card company (possibly $50,000 or more personal investment).

Business w/ High Risk of failure:
- Bio Chemical company
- Bio Tech Company
- Software Company
- License A Car Dealership
- Used Car Dealership
- Unsecured Credit Card Company
- Clothing Line
- Record Label
- Adult Business/Pornography- ***I wouldn't recom mend this one.***

An old friend once told me that you can't be poor and happy at the same time. Either you'll feel **secure** working a job for someone else and eventually grow content with just getting by. Or you may be a small business owner or highly educated –trained professional such as a doctor or lawyer and you will carve out a life of **comfortableness** and endure tremendous amounts of bad stress. Then there's the possibility of doing something that you love, while becoming very **wealthy** doing it. So which one do you desire to be? Secure, comfortable or wealthy? As my friend stared at me in contempt, already knowing what my answer was going to be- it was at that moment that I knew I wanted more. I wanted my own. I wanted my freedom and a more financially stable lifestyle.

With any business there are two things that people will remember about their experience:

- Level of Service
- Your name and Reputation

Therefore it is crucial that you present yourself as a professional and make sure your staff is courteous, prompt and knowledgeable in your field of business. The single most valuable and important resource that anyone has while acquiring wealth is Time. In today's ever changing global society- it is imperative that we utilize our time wisely and expediently.

Wealth is accumulated with a simple formula;
Money x Time = Profits.

Profits x Investments = Power.
Power (divided by) **Investments x Time = Wealth**

Money is a form of currency and can therefore be used as a resource, a form of leverage to build wealth. But money is not wealth. Money is simply a medium of exchange, a representation of value, the real commodity is the gold, silver, platinum, palladium or oil that guarantees/ insures the money medium. Before we move any further you need to understand the workings within the system of economics. Below are a few key terms that you will need to become familiar with. And we will cover more on banking in my next book, Open your Mind before you Invest.

Key Terms

Business: The purchase and sale of goods as an attempt to earn a profit.

Economics: The science that involves production, distribution and consumption of goods and services to propel a society's financial infra- structure.

Finance: Is the business of banking and investing, while managing revenues affecting the public economic system.

Capital Budget: A financial statement that estimates firms expenditures for major assets and its long term financing needs.

Capital Gains: the difference between a security's purchase price and its selling price. The amount of money from the sale of real estate or an investment.

Income Statement: a summary of a company's revenues and expenses during a certain time frame.

Working Capital: The difference between a company's current assets and current debt/ liabilities.

Revenue: the dollar amount earned by a company from providing services and business activities.

Profit: the dollar amount remaining after business expenses have been deducted from the revenue generated.

Net Income: Occurs when your company's revenues are more than the company's expenses.

Gross Profit: a company's accounting of total net sales minus the cost of goods sold.

Dividend: A payment of earnings to the stock holders of a corporate firm.

Corporation: S corp., C corp., or LLC company- all have the ability to act and function as a person within policy of the law. Often used as a shelter for most businesses, protects liability, assets and revenue streams of share-holders and investors. There are three different types of corporations.

Asset: the resources of value that a firm either own or control.

Expenditure: an amount of money spent, expenses incurred

Franchise: a form of business organization in which the owning group gives privilege to the use of their brand, products and services for profit, through a binding contract to an individual or group.

Franchisor: the owning group/ organization of all right a brand, business or service.

Franchisee: The individual or group being given the right to use and operate under a certain brand, business or service for profit.

- 6 -
Let's Talk Money

So now we know what wealth is and we also know where it is and who has it. It is now time to discuss how and what you need to do to get your share of the wealth pie. Unless you win the lottery or mega millions plan on working the rest of your life. Either you'll work for an employer and you will be at their mercy, or perhaps you'll work for yourself and become a small business owner. I sincerely hope that you also plan on being a savvy investor. There are many investments that can produce a modest ROI, some we will discuss later. So now that we've established that you must work- in some way or another, unless you plan on making minimum wage, you will need a formal education or become a skill's trade professional. Or, perhaps a savvy investor.

Remember, money is only a vehicle for us to use to obtain resources and assets. Although it's great to save money, you should also have a clear budget of what you want to retain and how much you want to spend, and of course keep the rest moving to gain more assets and resources. You can also benefit from significant tax shelters from your earnings versus expenditures, see your accountant or tax attorney for counsel. Remember money is a vehicle that we use to gain more assets and resources, that is the sole purpose for keeping the money moving into other lucrative investments. Whenever possible, always use other people's money to make your money, that's how you build credit, network and generate cash flow. And cash flow creates profits.

So now we have:
- Our business idea.
- And a rough business plan that we need to put on paper.
- We've chosen and met with our team- realtor, accountants, and lawyer (all free counsel of course).
- We have an idea of what wealth is and we know what money is truly used for and why—to get more resources.

It is now time for you to choose a lending institution to do your financial business. This is only one of many crucial steps to building wealth. You will want to select a bank or credit union that will give you a chance to establish yourself. Open up a checking account and test them out by applying for a small loan of perhaps 1,000 dollars or even apply for a 500 or 1,000 dollar credit card. Personally, I prefer to deal with small banks and credit unions because it seems as though the customer care is more sincere. You're a name with a smiling face- not just a number there, and that will enable you to build strong ties and networking.

You are looking for all types of cash to start your new business and I'm going to tell you where to look for it. From most to least likely to give you a loan for your new business, below are;

Viable Sources for Capital:

- **Local Credit Unions-** check around in your city and you will find the one that fit your needs. If you live in Michigan, try **Wanigas Credit Union.** If you live in Florida, try **Sun Coast Federal Credit Union.**

- **Small Business Administration-** log onto www.sba.gov . The SBA has several different loan programs for very specific reasons. So you must take your time and look through their programs and find the one best for your needs. However, I can assure you that the most common loan is the 7(a) Loan Program.

- **Angel Investors/ Investment firms-** often referred to as Angel Groups or Angel Networks, they are an excellent source- because they believe in your business and they don't want control, they only want a percentage of ownership –a fair share of future profits in exchange for their cash. Such firms are: www.Equitynet.com , www.fundingpost.com , www.midwestinvestmentnetwork.com and many more, search the web on Google.

- **Venture Capital Firms/ Investors-** these are investors that like to invest in biotech businesses, IT, software, hi technology and high risk businesses. Great source if your business falls within the high risk category that I previously mentioned. Some venture capital firms are: www.vcexpert.com , www.gobignetwork.com , www.fundable.com.

- **Mortgage brokerage-** borrow against equity

- **Government Grants-** the best and most secure and reliable source is www.usa.gov.

- **Banks-** Asset Backed Lending Loan. **Chase bank** is

usually very good with these types of loans and especially if real-estate or an automobile (five years old or newer to the current year) is involved as collateral.

- **Private Equity/ Investment Firm-** Although they will give you the cash, they also want controlling interest and management control.

So now that you have your sources and your strategy in place. There are some key things we must discuss before moving along any further. Below is what I call the ***red flag, danger-zone, double jeopardy*** wisdom for all aspiring business owners, small business owners and struggling business owners. So if you're a business losing money or a startup that's struggling to start you may find your answer here. Then you will have to evaluate your organization and make some adjustments.

THE MOST COMMON MISTAKES
START-UP's & SMALL BUSINESSES MAKE

- Failure to properly plan
- Lack of a creative and affordable marketing plan
- Failure to properly budget for unexpected expenses
- Prices are too high or too low
- Failure to secure capital for future overhead expenses for a minimum of one year
- Can't meet supply and demand
- Failure to manage company growth
- Poor management
- Failure to monitor company finances- (cash flow statement)
- Failure to attract new customers
- Poor Product or service

Here are some vital stats for you to remember. When things get rough and you feel like giving up, I want you to refer back to this page and these statistics.

- Out of 100 businesses – in the first year, 20 of them fail.
- In the next three years, of the 80 left, 35 of them will close down.

** Two years later, out of the 45 businesses remaining, 33 of them will go out of business.

*** In ten years 90 out of the 100 businesses will no longer exist.

Bankers, Investors and Supply stores are all going to be looking to see what kind of business you operate. Money is the least of your worries because if your start up plan and business structure is flawless than there's no cracks in your armor. When you are looking to raise money for your business, you become a sales person. Read my book, Sales Training Solutions to fine tune your skills. As a salesperson you want to overcome and clear up all objections in order to close the sale. The way we are going to handle those objections is by having a solid business plan addressing all concerns before they arise in the mind of the very ones considering giving you a business loan.

So What Do Bankers look for?
- Credit Management: Do you pay your bills on time
- Stability and Geographic's: How long have you been in business, where is it located, and how much experience do you have in your business field?
- Demographics: Is there a market for what you are attempting to do? And when is the expected ROI?

- Income: How much you are asking for? And will your company generate enough income to pay it back? What assets does your company currently have?

Types of Financing for you to think about, I described each in the above fore mentioned. Please take your time to consider your options. And don't be afraid to ask questions when you do not understand something.

- Owner financing
- Debt Financing
- Equity Financing
- Trade and/ or Credit

- 7 -
Understanding Corporations and Business Structures

Every business needs an organizational structure, a way that clearly defines your business operations, decision makers and owners. Some people simply get a small business license and run everything in their own name. And for some people and businesses that's absolutely fine. However if you want to grow your business and obtain mass amounts of wealth and power and pass that on to your children and grandchildren, then a corporation may be perfect for your business. Corporations offer a variety of benefits to any business owner. Let's discuss the different type of business entities you can form and some of advantages and disadvantages as well.

Type of Business:

Sole Proprietorship- This simply means this is a business with one owner. This is the most common type of business organization used in America. And for decades it was also the back bone of America.

Pro: Very easy to start, a small business license and a license for whatever you're selling and your taxes will be fairly simple as well because all income from the business will be considered your personal income. Typically, this is a very good organization for a small business. You also reap all of the rewards, the profits.

Negative: You are tied to your business and your business to you. So if someone sues you as a person, guess what? They can also take the assets from your business and potentially bankrupt you. You're not protected with a sole proprietorship. You also pay more taxes and receive no tax benefits.

• Note: you can start off as a sole proprietor but when the business gets rolling and you start making money you should probably consider forming a corporation. The Type of corporation will all depend upon your needs, taxes and funding.

Type of Business:

Partnership- A partnership is just that; an agreement between two or more parties. The partnership is very similar in organizational form to the sole proprietorship being that the partnership is not a separate legal entity and offers the partners virtually no tax breaks or protection from liability. However, partnerships are effective because it splits the work load as well as the risk for all parties. Not all partners are equal. As such, the profits may not be split equally either. Most Partnerships are structured under an LLC or limited liability corporation. An LLC is very inexpensive to form. It's also very simple to raise capital by selling points (or percentages) of the business interest. As such, an LLC can have an unlimited amount of owners.

Pro: Unlike a sole proprietorship, a partnership can actually carry debt and property in its own name as an entity of its own. Is passed through similar to a corporation, except it is shown on the partners taxes, must file Form 1065 with the IRS.

Negative: A partner or all partners can be held responsible for the mistakes or civil/criminal actions of the other partners; this drawback increases the risk of personal liability for all parties involved. Also once taxes are passed through to the owner's personal tax, the tax bracket increases and the owners may be taxed at a higher rate.

Corporations- There are two main types of corporations; C Corporation and S Corporation. Before we get into the different types of corporations, first let's understand why corporations were created and how they are used. Initially, corporations were created for the sole purpose of doing what the sole proprietor and the partnership wasn't capable of, which is the corporation can act as a separate legal entity. It can stand alone, therefore it can be sued. It can also have and build credit, own property and make investments. But the major benefit of a corporation is that it protects the shareholders (owners of the stock that controls the corporation) and in most cases the company's administration and board of directors from any liability in the event of a lawsuit or negligent action. And the prime and final advantage to incorporating is the ***incredible tax benefits*** you will receive, as long as you have a very good accountant. Now let's understand the differences between the C and S corporations.

C Corporation:

The "C" Corporation is a, ***for profit*** organization, which means it was designed to generate income and make a profit. The majority of people who own a small business also work for their business as a manager or employee; therefore a C corporation would be ideal because the salaries and bonuses that the corporation pays its employees can be used to receive substantial tax breaks. If the corporation can show a zero profit on its income statement and income tax statement because the corporation paid its employees, your corporation may qualify to not pay any corporate tax to the IRS. However, if the corporation makes a profit it will have to pay corporate taxes but at a much lower tax rate than an individual tax rate. Check with your local accountant for specific tax information.

S Corporation:

An S corporation is limited to 35 shareholders. An S corporation is taxed by the IRS like a partnership; it (the s corp.) passes its profits and losses through to the owners' (shareholders). Therefore, the corporation doesn't file taxes but instead it files an informational tax return known as File Form 1120S. And the shareholders reflect the profit and/ or losses on their individual tax returns.

* Please note that most companies hardly ever use their own name. They usually file for a DBA at their local county clerk's office. DBA simply means 'Doing Business As'. It's a license that allows you to operate your business as whatever fictitious name that you choose. The cost for a DBA is usually between 10 and 50 dollars depending on where you file.

I am only giving you a foundation to build upon. You have to put forth the effort to study. You will have to use a tremendous amount of energy building your business. You will be rejected by so many people that you will feel like giving up. You will make mistakes along the way. But that's okay, you will learn, grow and then teach from our mistakes. But don't ever quit. This book is designed to be a quick read and great reference for those that want to grow. Use it as a guide and a platform.

**Also when you form any type of corporation the government will give you a T.I.N (also known as E.I.N.), which stands for Tax Identification Number (or Employee Identification Number). Think of this as your company's very own social security number. This is how your company will be able to stand on its own and generate credit.

- 8 -
What if You Have Bad Credit?

If you have bad credit things may be very challenging and quite difficult but not impossible. A person with bad credit has to pay astronomically higher interest rates, face tighter pre qualifications by producing more documents for proof of income to top lenders, and often get approved for less money than you applied for and on a shorter term for the loan to be repaid. All of these situations often put the business owner (the borrower) into an even more financially stressed situation. My advice is if you have bad credit and you desire to start a business, your primary goal before starting any type of business is to build your personal credit. After all, who wants a business partner that doesn't pay their bills? I'm going to share a few suggestions on how to repair your credit. The very first thing you need to do is request a copy of your credit report from all three credit reporting agencies; Equifax, Experian and Transunion. You may be able to have certain items removed by simply writing a dispute letter. Consult with a credit counselor to find out more specifics. Credit counselors charge a fee for their service but they are very effective because they help educate the consumer as you learn how to establish credit and manage money responsibly. Most financial advisors recommend that you review your credit report once a year for errors. You are entitled to one free credit report every year from the three major credit reporting agencies.

The type of things that credit reporting agencies collect about you is the same information that lenders and bankers look at when deciding rather or not to give you a loan. Therefore, it is crucial that you keep a close eye on your credit and manage it properly, try not to over extend yourself. Budget your money by paying your bills first and then yourself second. I know that it's easier said than done. But remember I'm telling you these things from experience, so I know that it can be obtained. So, what information do credit reporting agencies collect from and on us?

1. Detailed list of your creditors within the past 5 to 7 years
2. Your payment history with those creditors
3. Your place of employment and length of time there
4. Your date of birth
5. Current residence and length of time at residence
6. Your social security number
7. All of your debts, including student loans
8. Judgments' from a lawsuit
9. Wage garnishments
10. Bankruptcies
11. Fore closures & Tax liens.

There are alternatives other than credit counseling and money management firms. If you own a home, you can always try a consolidation loan. But I would advise against doing that because there are penalties accrued on top of the loan and if you can't make the payments you may lose your property. The bottom line is do not take on more debt than you can handle. And if you are at the bottom, I've given you the blue print on how you can rise. Bankruptcy is a form of debt management but it should be your very last resort. A Bankruptcy will wipe out all credit card debt, stop foreclosures, wage garnishments, auto repossessions and stop creditors from contacting you. A bankruptcy can follow you for over 10 years. It can prevent you from buying a motor home, a residential home, a car and in some cases hinder you from gainful employment. However, there are circumstances where a person is forced to make that decision to become debt free. Although not all debts are erased when you file bankruptcy, for example; student loans cannot be filed upon, even after the bankruptcy you are liable to repay your student loan debt. Also you cannot file on child support, alimony support, government fines, or federal court imposed fees and taxes.

There are two different types of bankruptcies:
Chapter 7 and Chapter 13.

A chapter 7 bankruptcy is when you have the sole intent of erasing all debt. You must liquidate all of your assets, except for the items, loans and property that you want to reaffirm on. To reaffirm simply means that you are going to keep the property or loan and continue to make payments on it. Things such as cars, tools and credit cards can all be reaffirmed. Other items and property may be sold by the court appointed bank-ruptcy trustee. After you file and all business is settled by the court you will receive a full discharge of your debts.

A chapter 13 bankruptcy is slightly different than a chapter 7. The chapter 13 gives you a scheduled repayment plan to repay all creditors over the course of five years or less. When you file chapter 13 you get to keep your property, even though you are technically in default of your financial obligation. The bankruptcy consolidates all of your expenses/ creditors and gives you the protection from creditors and the flexibility to get back on your feet.

- 9 -
Money Management
Rules for Success

1. Successful people don't buy consumer goods on credit,
    they pay in cash! Consumer goods are things like furniture,
    electronics, appliances and jewelry.
2. Successful people do not; buy durable goods on credit such
    as boats, RV's, planes and jets, even luxury or sports cars.
    If you can't pay cash… you cannot afford to have them.
3. Successful people don't diversify their portfolios. Instead
    they focus on building one business at a time. Don't be a
    scatter brain trying to do too many things and taking on too
    much at once.
4. Successful People build strong, supportive teams around
    them;
    a. Attorney (corporate, tax, real estate)
    b. Accountant
    c. Banker
    d. Insurance broker
    e. Bond company
** Make sure that your team is young and ambitious with
contacts to make moves for you.

Since we know that money is simply a resource that we utilize to make profits, please understand that credit is the leverage used to propel the world of business and finance. Successful people only use credit to make more money and churn more profits. It is also just as important that you understand the differences between good debt and bad debt.

Financial Management isn't something that you are born to do; it isn't inherited, nor is it genetically passed along. Financial management involves the understanding of money. You must be able to not only figure out the best possible way to raise capital for the company, but you must also stay within the projected budget of your company to ensure a profit. Think of your house hold as a company. If you can properly manage your personal finances and successfully maintain your household with a positive cash flow, then you may be ready to start your own business.

Examples of Good debt vs Bad debt:

Good Debt	Bad Debt
Office (inside your home) that you lease out to your company.	Home if you live in it, no office/ business. You pay a mortgage get no tax breaks that make it a liability.
Rental property providing a positive monthly/ annual ROI	A refinance loan
Short term loan to fund business needs, ROI in 90 days	Any consolidation loan
Car that has a loan on it and is making money for you Daily, weekly, monthly	A car that has a loan on it and is your personal vehicle
An RV used for business and capital gain, or as a second home (can get a tax break end of year)	An RV used for personal recreation/ not for business.
Credit card with a low or zero balance	Credit card with a high balance or maxed out.

Successful People are dynamic in the field of business because they never stop learning. Successful people are also very competent and never over promise and under deliver. They stay professional and always keep a watchful eye on good investments and never make a move without a solid investment strategy. Successful people never take on too much bad debt; know how to create good debt and when to leverage it. Successful people understand that risk is simply a part of doing business. Below is a list of good investments vs. bad investments;

Good Investments:
- Gold, silver, and all other precious metals.
- Government Bonds (if over 10 years maturity)
- Bank CD (certificate of deposit)
- 401K through your employer or IRA offered by a bank. This is perfect if you are self-employed, own a business, or can't invest in a 401k through your employer. An IRA stands for investment retirement account. It is very similar to a 401k. Check with your local banker for details.
- Duplex rental property or 3 bed room single family home (if you can keep them rented with good on time paying renters.)
- Mutual funds that invest in oil, green technology, and people's needs such as diapers, water, and personal products.

Bad Investments:
- Land Contracts
- Stock market (the stock market is like a Vegas Casino crap shoot or slot machine. You'll probably have better odds in Vegas than on Wall Street).
- Farming or Cattle (unless you have experience in this field, I suggest you stay away. Medical bills for animals, nature destroying the crops, repairs for equipment, and licenses can very well bankrupt you).
- Pyramid schemes (offering to make you an IBO- independent business owner)

- A start-up internet business (unless it has solid advertising or associated with a reputable company or brand you may run into problems).
- A start up Clothing Line (even with a big name behind you and lots of money, you still may not break through. Trends change and people sometimes don't adapt).

All of the things that I have shared with you mean absolutely nothing and you will get nothing if your credit isn't good. And also if you do not have a solid plan that includes a solid budget. But most importantly, if you do not believe in your heart that you can succeed than all of this is will mean absolutely nothing.

Credit is more important today than it ever has been in our country's history. Due to recent changes within the banking industry since over the past ten years as of this writing (2014) there has been a decrease in the number of banks, credit unions, and Mortgage Company's due to mergers, buy-outs, improper use of funds, poor management and government interference. As a result there is more government regulation of the entire banking industry. The Patriot Act ensures that all financial institutions collect thorough background information on all new accounts. So it is very important to make sure that your credit is solid. It is equally important to write down your goals. Start with your short term or 6 month goal then write down your 1 year goal and 5 year goal and 10 year goals. The purpose for writing them down is to re enforce the thought, the desire and drive that you can accomplish them. It's motivation in its purest form.

- 10 -
How to Properly Structure
Your Business Plan

When writing your business plan there isn't any room for errors so therefore make sure it is professional, well thought out and sincere. Below are the headings or captions of each section that a proper business plan should contain.

1. **Executive Summary-** This is the single most important aspect of your business plan because it gives the investors an understanding of the scope of your business, main purpose, and the business primary goals. It also encompasses the future plans for the company and history of the business owners. You should also create your mission statement. A mission statement discusses the reason you want to start this business- it's your passion or whatever your personal desire is to start this business. Also in the mission statement share your immediate thoughts and future goals.

2. **Products and Services-** This section discusses the type of products that your business will sell. Be sure to express why your product is a good idea. Discuss how you intend to brand your product and how (or what methods) you

intend to use to sell your product. Tell why you believe that your product or service is unique. Also discuss who your competition is, where your competition is located, why your product or service can take a certain percentage of the competitions market.

3. **Advertising and Marketing-** You should be very clear and concrete with your ideas of how you intend to let the world know that your business exists and that you are open for business. Its simple promotions. And there are many different resources that you can use to promote your company. The internet and social media, radio, trade publications, television and conventional word of mouth.

4. **Financing-** Investment, Expenses, Profit! These three words are crucial in this part of your business plan. This is your chance to thoroughly explain why you need the investment; how do you plan to use the money; and potential profit. Also explain how much you have invested thus far into this business. If you have not made an investment in your own business, why would anyone want to?

5. **Management Team and Staff-** In this particular section introduce yourself and your management team. State why you and your staff are qualified to run the business. Some people even include a professional resume.

6. **Sales Projections-** Depending on what business professional you are talking with, this section may be referred to by several different names; Sales Forecast, Profit and Statement, or Financial Projections. Regardless of the title,

the content and format typically remain the same. In this section explain the goals of the company and explain how the business will get a return on investment. State a realistic number (based on your research) how much of your product or service that you think you will sell. This should be broken down in three stages; 1st year sales projections, 5year sales projections, and 10 year sales goals and expansion plans. If you can provide a profit and loss statement for each phase, this will only benefit your vision and increase the investor's willingness to invest. You can do your own profit and loss statement with QuickBooks. But I advise you to see an accountant, if you can afford it.

7. **Contact Information-** Provide the business address. If your business does not have an address yet then provide your home address. Include your email, company website, and business phone number and your cell phone number.

I've given you a spring board into the world of business. There is so much more than what I've discussed that you must learn. But most of what you need will come from experience. You will make mistakes along the way. You will feel like a failure at times. You will have doubts lingering in your mind. That's okay because those are the things every great person overcomes. It is through adversity that we grow stronger and smarter. Never stop learning, always stay humble, and always respect everyone.

- 11 -
Appearance is Everything

Most times it is not the lack of knowledge that hinders people from reaching their best and gaining success, for it is a person's behavior, tone, and vocabulary that halt all progress and positive growth. Having the right behavior means having the right attitude. The right attitude means being capable mentally to withstand the pressures and hardships that life will bring about. It means that you possess the fortitude (the drive) to physically and mentally accomplish the goals that you have set. Nothing comes to a sleeper but dreams, and nothing comes to a procrastinator but wasted time and missed opportunities. Wake up, look up, thank the Lord and get up! I encourage you to find your untapped potential to become your very best self.

Untapped potential is what you are but cannot see, touch, or hear. It's who we are beneath your subconscious. It's who we are if we can believe in God and ourselves. But believing is meaningless with premium effort. In other words, get up off of your behind and work until the plan happens. And then work some more!

I know what you are going through. I have experienced the pain of having no money; no saving's account, no food, and no place to live. Yes, I've been homeless before, when I lived in

Las Vegas. I know the gut-wrenching, head busting, heart-ache of trying to hold on to do the right thing. I know the agony of not knowing if you will survive. And those were the times that I got down on my knees and prayed. Then I picked up my Bible and it was *Faith* that got me through. She's an angel from God that has never let me down.

Ephesians Chapter 2 verse 8-9; "for it is by grace you have been saved through faith. And this is not your own doing; it is the gift of God, not a result of works, so that no one may boast." Throughout history the word faith has been used to conquer nations and build empires. And we are going to need faith to build our empires as well.

I'm not telling you to become a Baptist, Pentecostal, Later-day Saints, Jehovah's Witness, Catholic, Hindu, Jewish, or any of the Islamic sects of religion. Whatever you decide that's your right and your business. But what I am telling you is that in order to be a successful person and a righteous person you will need some type of spirituality as a platform in your life. You will also need *Patience*. Patience is often talked about but seldom practiced. It's easy to verbally use the word; however the challenge is to actually exercise patience, to actually go through the motion of waiting out time in real life situations. So how do we get patience and where does it exist? Patience exists within the mind of our bodies and it lives within our souls. It is an angel and a gift from God. Patience can't be gained or developed unless you put on the cloak of Wisdom. Besides Love, Wisdom is the most precious gift that anyone could ever receive from God. Here's what the scripture says about Wisdom; "Wisdom calls aloud in the street, she raises her voice in the public squares; at the head of the noisy streets she cries out, in the gate ways of the city she makes her speech perfect." Proverbs Chapter 1 verses 20-21. In Proverbs Chapter 2 Verse 10, "For Wisdom will enter your heart and knowledge will be pleasant to your soul." And Proverbs Chapter 2 verse 12 solidifies the importance of Wisdom, "Wisdom will save you from the ways of the wicked men, from men whose words are perverse." The point is that wisdom is pure and cannot be tainted. Wisdom is the under- standing of supreme self-awareness and knowledgeable enough to know that all great teachers are constant students. As you embrace Wisdom you will develop the knowledge of others and how to deal with each situation. Wisdom opens the doors to the supreme science of the galaxies, the universe, stars and the mastering of every living creature within it. Scriptures' throughout the Bible constantly refer to Faith, Patience, Love, Wisdom and Under-standing as females (she or her).

Faith, Patience, Love, Wisdom, and Understanding are all spirits, but they are also gifts from the Lord God. They were there in the beginning, before the earth was formed. Genesis Chapter 1 verse 26; God said " Let us make man in our image, in our likeness, and let them rule over the fish of the sea and the birds of the air, over livestock, all over the earth and over all creatures that move along the ground." [New International version]. So the lingering question is, who was God talking to when he said "our image, our likeness"? Was it the Angels Gabriel and Michael, Jesus, or someone else? Perhaps it was a female?

Before the very existence of time, Faith, Patience, Love, Wisdom and Understanding were there with God. And they will be here long after we're gone because they're infinite and have no boundaries within time and each of those gifts are priceless, supremely profound and will magnify your life in ways that you've only dreamed of. But it all starts with faith. Faith is to not only believe but it also requires action. Believe in yourself and your abilities and believe in your family. Believe in Jesus Christ, that he died for all of our sins and that there's no better fixer than God. There's no better love than the love of God. And once you believe, only then will you begin to do God's will. I promise you that once you begin to do God's will life will become much more rewarding.

I often ponder the tumultuous journey that I've traveled in my life. Man, has it been one hell of a ride! The way that I measure my level of success is by looking at previous years as a comparison to what I'm doing now. I evaluate myself to keep my life and the people in my life in proper perspective, in order to keep what's important to me in front of me. As I reflect, sometimes I can still hear the loud clanking sound of air compressed doors slamming behind me, the sound of jail. I can even remember walking into the prison intake room and stripping down to nudity. But I refused to be stripped of my dignity. So as I prepared myself for war, I knew that I was in for the long haul. I stared out of the prison window at the sea of inmates moving about on the yard, truth entered my heart and I began to see things clear. I needed God.

In the first chapter, I expressed how I idolized Michael Jordan simply because I was amazed by his level of skill. He is the greatest to ever play the game of basketball. But what made Michael Jordan so great? It's no secret that he was blessed with a tremendous amount of talent, but what made Michael so special and unique was his ability to overcome. He endured the adversity and brutal physical punishment of the Detroit Pistons led by Isiah Thomas and then by the bruising New York

Knicks led by Patrick Ewing. Besides, having to defeat the best to become the best, he had to learn to adapt and grow as a leader. Michael Jordan never knew that he would win all of those champion- ships but he went into those games with a goal, with a clear focus- the killer instinct- and the will to win. The same holds true in real life and business situations, we must be ready for that moment. We must find the will power and mental forti- tude, as well as be able to tap into it; take it to the next level in order to achieve greatness.

There will be times that you have doubt. Fear will set in and you will feel as if you can't go on anymore. There will be days that you feel like giving up. But remember the killer instinct. Don't give up! Try an alternative. Take a different road. Tap into that will power and keep your eyes on what's in front of you. I encourage you to be relentless in life to bring out the best in yourself and your family.

I have witnessed God's mercy and I've experienced his grace, and so have many of you but you probably didn't recognize Him. The scripture reads; "For the grace of God that brings salvation has appeared to all men. It teaches us to say no to ungodliness and world passions and to live self-controlled, upright and Godly lives in this present age." Titus Chapter 2 verses 11 and 12.

I assume the most of you are probably reading this chapter and wondering why I'm discussing Bible scriptures and talking about the greatness of Michael Jordan. Even though both of those subjects are quite enjoyable to me, my reasoning is far more logical. I am giving you tools and building blocks from the Bible that you will need along your journey in life and business. I am using Michael as an example of the drive, never give up attitude, and the killer instinct. Those three traits paired with execution equals results. However you will never get any solid positive results if you don't take on a new appearance.

It is true that appearance is everything; it is also relevant to know that we must build our inner core to help give our spirits a new appearance. And only then can we walk in the light and *Love* of God. Putting on the cloak of wisdom will give us the mental toughness that we need to become great. Success is yours for the taking. But first there are a few key elements that we must be aware of that will enable us to progress to the next level in this life, and the next.

1. Seize the moment- Seizing the moment requires a certain level of understanding about life, business and other situations. It's a level of foresight to know when the time is right and that the time is now. Sometimes the moment comes later and you must know when to exercise patience and wait. Time is the one thing that none of us can control. Due to our lack of control over time, is the reason why time is so precious. Time has no conscience, it cannot think. It dictates without a will. Time has no measure of its existence. Sure as the day comes, and the night falls the seasons will change and everything will be done in time. So that is why knowing when to seize the moment is so important. For most, it's a skill that will flourish as you go throughout life's experiences, and for others, well, they may never get it and of course they will attempt to capture the moment when time has expired.

2. Dress with self Esteem- You don't have to dress distasteful or inappropriate to be seen, just as you don't have to yell to be heard. So ladies try wearing clothes that fit and that aren't so revealing. If you change the image you are projecting, you will also change the type of men that are approaching you. Ladies, dress like you respect yourself and you'll find that men in particular will start to do the same. And guys pull your pants up, stop sagging; lose the ice platinum and gold grills, try wearing clothes that fit your frame, it's time to man up. I'm sure you wouldn't wear a bathing suit to go skiing. Or you wouldn't wear a fur coat on a Florida beach in the middle of July. The same is true with in life in general; you wear the proper attire according to the setting you are attending.

3. Foul Language- The mouth speaks what the heart is full of. We have to clean up our language to become a better person. Language is the means of communication through signs, symbols and speech to express thoughts, feelings, and actions. The type language that we use identifies who we are. Our vocabulary and language gives people a general idea or synopsis of our character as well. Based on the type of words that we use, we give insight of our intentions and our level of thinking. The use of curse words or degrading language only shows society how shallow your mental capacity really is. It also signifies that you are incapable of expressing yourself with the slightest bit of intelligence. Please don't misunderstand me; I'm aware that the harsh experiences of life can be a very devastating and damaging. I believe, because of our experiences we should strive to become better instead of giving up and becoming complacent. Why are you a thug when you can be a realtor, doctor, or banker? Why become a gangster when you can become a counselor, accountant, business investor, stockbroker or sales professional. You can be whatever your heart desire. But you must put your mind into focus to conquer your dream.

- 12 -
My Personal Winning Sales Techniques

Sales is the road in which wealth is built. Every business is in sales; either the business offers a service, a product, or sometimes both. By design the owners and senior managers net the wealth and keep the riches, while the entry level staff or lower level associates' of the company can barely pay their bills on time. That's truly a very unfair and greedy way of doing business. Where's the gratitude to the labor force that helped propel you to success? It's no secret that sales are the backbone of America. Free enterprise and free trade are the cornerstones that make this country so great. Having a republic with a free market creates an economy that continues to evolve. But it all starts and end with a sale.

Because we are all entrepreneurs, I decided to share the techniques that I've used over the years that have made me a successful sales person and business owner. Inside this chapter you will find sales scripts, proper meet and greet techniques, resources to generate more sales leads, cold calling scripts, proper and improper word tracks and so much more. Although in my scripts I am selling cars and RV's the process is essentially the same. Whether you are selling AT&T u verse services, shoes, clothes, hats, or food my processes never change. The product or service is inter-changeable and the script is designed as a guide to assist in getting you *onto the road to the sale.*

Professional Sales Training Program

Do you have a clear vision?

Key Benefits:
- New and Fresh sales techniques for sales professionals
- How to ask the right qualifying questions
- The best and proper word tracks for phone,
internet and in person
- How to generate solid leads and turn more leads into sales
- Offer great closing tools and marketing strategies-
other than the internet

Sales Training Program

Lesson 1: Steps to the Sale

Everyone knows about the traditional and old fashion road to the sale. Although each steps may vary somewhat slightly. The same 12 steps have been etched and laminated in the minds of most car sales people. Some dealerships have made it a requirement for the sales people to carry the steps to the sale in their pocket. Well let's list the original 12 steps to the sale and see if the times that we are living in allow for such steps to help us become successful sales people.

Step 1:	Meet and greet	Still very effective
Step 2:	Gather Information/ Qualify	Not very effective, people today are apprehensive to give information out so quickly.
Step 3:	Select a Vehicle	Still very effective
Step 4:	Present vehicle features and Demo ride	Not very effective. You have wowed the customer with a bunch of technology, confused them more and then rushed them on a test drive.

Step 5   Trial Close   Not very effective because of the comparisons and choices today, buyers are shoppers. Make sure you have your customer in the right vehicle before you attempt to close them.

Step 6:   Trade in Evaluation/   Not very effective if you
            Walk around: don't have them in the right car. Or if you haven't been given enough information to fully qualify your customer to understand their needs.

Step 7:   Write Up

Step 8:   Present #'s

Step 9:   Negotiate

Step 10:   Manager Turn   } Not Effective
            over/ Close

Step 11:   Finance and Insurances
            Turn Over

Step 12:   Schedule Delivery/Spot

So let's shred those old, or shall I say more traditional methods and habits that we often use while talking to our peers and our customers. The reason why steps 7 thru 12 are not effective is because you lost your customer in Step number 4. Even though they are going on a demo ride in their minds they are already thinking of an escape route from you, a way for them to break free and shop some more. So therefore you must be confident in your ability as sales professionals. Next you must properly qualify your customers. That way you will prevent them from thinking of a way to get away from you after the demo ride. I'm going to show you how to qualify your customers while keeping an open dialog. **So are you ready professionals? Let's go!**

<u>Fresh Steps to the Sale</u>

Step 1: Proper Meet & Greet (*will cover in lesson 2*)

Step 2: Offer Information, Make suggestions, Exercise Critical thinking- The customer will start giving you information. Keep an open dialog going, ask your customers' questions that lead to a benefit for them. Such as "Will a five passenger SUV get you the gas mileage and comfort you need?" and "What other type of information can I offer you?" Keep offering infor- mation. Inform customers of your dealerships specials and rebates. Sell yourself and the dealership by being armed with Product Knowledge, while gathering information to properly qualify your customer.

Step 3: Ask about the trade in-Take interest in the customer. Ask the owners to tell you about their car. Drop the tradeoff to be evaluated and get back to your customer. <u>Don't leave your customer alone for too long.</u> Always stay with them and follow through with confidence.

Step 4: Introduce customer to Inventory- (while trade is being evaluated). Most customers today know what they want and how much they're willing to spend. Be thorough with your product presentation- I want you to go with the customer on a test drive. While on the test drive I want you to mention three key features that the customer should notice while driving; turning ratio, comfortable seating and roomy for long road trips, shock absorbers, or the technology. The key is to engage the customer with conversation so they subconsciously notice the benefits of what you've told them. You want to psychologically lead your customer to the sale. Engage your customer (while on the test-drive, as your heading back to the dealership) ask the customer one of three questions.

Three questions pertaining to the options and benefits you mentioned on the test drive.

Such as:

Question 1: Was the turning ratio as great as I promised?

Question 2: It has great gas mileage and plenty of interior room; does this vehicle fulfill your needs?

Question 3: Are you interested in getting more information about this vehicle?

* If the answer is yes to any of these questions, write the deal up.

Step 5: Write up- get your customer comfortable, offer them a seat, and relax their mood by getting them some refreshments.

Step 6: Present the figures and close your customer- As you walk back to your desk say; "I hope I wasn't gone too long?" "We just have a few more details to go over and then you can take your new vehicle home." Present the numbers.

*Customer is upset and/ or reject the numbers, don't like the deal.

Stay in your seat. Do not panic. Do not lose control of your customer. Calm yourself and then make eye contact with your customer. Reassure them of your professionalism and willingness to deal within reason. Keep working the deal and write down what the customer is requesting.

Step 7: Close your customer- The goal is to make a sale. The customer is buying from you because they like you. So why get out of your seat and run for help to a manager that is a stranger to the customer? Each time you get up and run to the manager's desk, you lose power and your chances to close the sale diminish greatly. STAY IN YOUR SEAT. Close the customer on their terms, write down their offer, repeat their terms, and shake their hand and say, congratulations. Get a down payment from the customer right now and tell them that's the only way to convince your manager of the deal. Money speaks volumes. Now get up and take the offer to your manager.

--If you can't get an offer or you can't close them. Tell them that you would like to show them something and say, "Follow me". Give them a tour of the dealership. The very last person on that tour that your customer will meet is your floor manager/ the closer. Introduce the customer to the closer and be quiet. The closer will do their own information gathering and eventually lead them back to your desk, at which point the real objections and customer reservations are put on the table. It is essential to have a psychologically strong, yet also savvy person as your closer.

Dealerships: The type of closer you will need is of intelligence and integrity, not rude or obnoxious. You want a hammer but one that hits you without you knowing you've been hit.

After the closer has finished, it's their job and yours to make introduction to finance.

Step 8: Finance and Insurance Turn over (F& I t/o)

Step 9: Delivery Process- *according to your local dealer*

** Manager's trust your sales staff; don't be an idiot, take the mini deals and the flats. Those few sales are better than no sales at all.

Rate your level of sales, which sales personality are you?

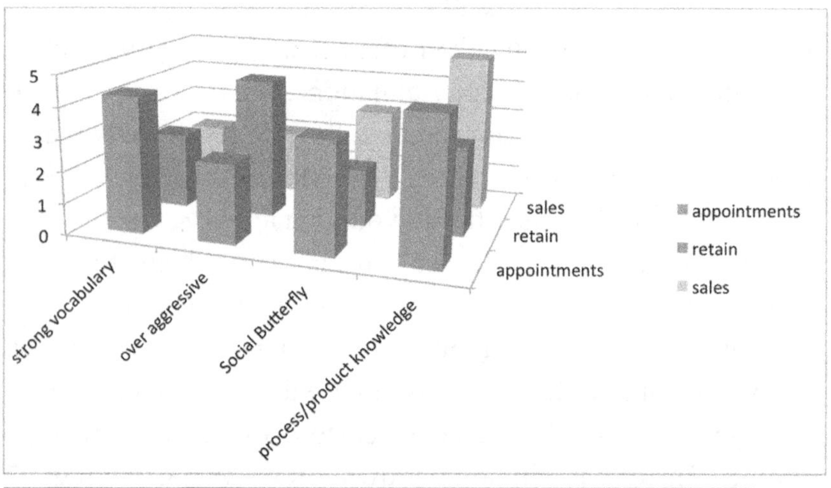

Type of Sales Person	Appointments Front column	Retain Middle column	Sales Back column
strong vocabulary	4.3	2.4	2
over aggressive	2.5	4.4	2
Social Butterfly	3.5	1.8	3.5
process/product knowledge	4.5	2.8	5

• Numbers are based on every 10 customers that the sales person meet or come in contact with.

Proper Meet & Greet

Lesson 2: Meet & Greet Scripts,
Improper Word tracks, Effective Closing Tracks

We're going to explore different techniques regarding proper and effective ways to greet a customer. If you greet a customer properly they will remember you and in most cases will buy from you, if not immediately, give it some time.

The first thing we do when we come to work is check our personal life at the door. We are now a chameleon, a shape shifter. So SMILE! ALWAYS SMILE!

Greeting 1: **"Good (time of day it is- morning, noon, evening). Welcome to (your dealership). I'm (your first and last name). And you are?"** REACH OUT AND SHAKE THEIR HAND.
Sales Person {ask them}: **"What type of information are you looking for today?"**
* have plenty of energy in your voice. This type of greeting is a classic soft sale.

Greeting 2: Sales Person: **"Hello I'm (your name) and you are?"** (Extend your hand)
"Mr. (Customer's name), we appreciate your business today." Customer response: "I haven't given you my business yet." Salesperson: **"What type of information can I offer to you?"**
** This type of dialogue engages the customer and subtlety plant seeds to the sale.

Greeting 3: **"Welcome to (your dealership's name), We appreciate the fact that you came out to our big sale today. Which vehicle interested you most?"**

*** This type of greeting is very direct but pleasant. It puts you at ease; gains control and leads the customer to the sale.

Improper Word Tracks

Never ever say the following things. If you want to sale more of whatever you sale, erase the negative jargon. The old saying; never say never is true in sales.

1. Never use the word "never".
2. If the terms are agreeable would you take it today?
3. What can we do to earn your business today?
4. Can we put this together today?
5. How much money can you put down?
6. Can you put any money down?
7. What are you thinking?
8. What ya think?
9. Can't Won't
10. Don't
11. No
12. No way
13. Not possible
14. Will not (won't)
15. Wouldn't
16. Shouldn't
17. Couldn't
18. Is not (Isn't)

Effective Closing Tracks

1. "The payment is reasonable. Being that it makes perfectly good sense to upgrade now. Excellent thinking and congratulations on your decision. I'll get the vehicle ready for you now." **(Stand up, shake their hand and start the delivery process).**

2. "Other than the…(price, color, the scratch-whatever) This seems to be the perfect car for you. Thank you for your business. Let me inform my manager that we have earned your business."

3. "Great news I have an approval. The bank is requesting a small down payment. Typically the lenders like to see the customer invest at least 10% down. How close are you to that amount?

4. (Grab the credit application)

"Whose name will the vehicle be titled in? And your social security # is ?..... Let's complete our paperwork to get the best approval."

Can you think of any other effective closing tracks? Write them down.

____

____

____

____

____

How and what to Sell

Lesson 3:   3E's, Generating leads, R.A.P. Customers, Goal Setting, Cold Call Scripts

In the 21st century with all of the technology out there you cannot sell anyone anything! You can't sell me a washer, a dryer, clothes, jewelry, cars, trucks, not even sex. Most people only pay for those objects because they desire or lust them on their own terms, psychologically. So therefore if a person doesn't want what you're offering then you don't and can't make a sale, thus, reinforcing the fact that you can't sell anyone anything. However, you can offer information. You can also offer great service, a great product and commitment to honesty. Sometimes those things make money, sometimes they don't. But we are here to make money- and to make money make us more money.

So, if you can't sell what you've been hired to sell? What can you sell?

- Yourself; your charm, smile, wit and winning personality
- The dealership
- The Professionalism

* The price is going to be what it is. Someone is always going to be cheaper down the road. And even further down the road, someone is cheaper than the previous guy. So let's not make price a factor.

I want to you to meet the three E's.

Energy, Excitement, Entertainment

They're sisters and they are going to help you take the focus off of price and instead you will build value in your product, yourself, the dealership and the professionalism in which the sale is handled.

Energy; You must stay motivated and on your feet. Smile, but don't look silly. Positive voice inflection is always a bonus. Sound normal but be very enthused. Your customer will feel your vibe and it will rub off. Take notes on your note pad when your customer is talking. It leaves a positive impression.

Excitement; Be passionate about whatever you're talking about. Speak with genuine interest, take concern and be willing to go the extra mile to prove that you are worthy of the sale. Just like yawning, happiness is contagious. If you are excited, even the grumpiest customer will lighten up.

Entertainment; Sales people, laughter always lightens the mood, but tread lightly, some customers may find certain jokes or stories offensive. So use your best judgment and read your customer's personality. But light humor at your clumsiness, good/clean upbeat music, buying the customer a soda, giving them free popcorn, giving the kids balloons and coloring books, buying the customer lunch or delivering the car to the customer's home is all considered forms of entertainment.

Dealerships and dealer principles

You should have something going on at least 3 to 4 times a week, such as: Red Cross blood drive, Cub Scout or Girl Scout sale, Rotary gathering or meeting, invite the food on wheels truck to sell barbeque and pay the radio station for a live session to air it, as you slash prices, or hold an after hours event like an amateur fight night or celebrity signing and promote it. These are just examples that should give you some sort of spark. People, I want you to get creative and think outside the box. Think of some events that can be held throughout the week at your dealership. Think of any and everything. These events are designed to bring in traffic. Traffic creates new leads. New leads turn into potential customers.

We must **R.A.P.** every potential customer in order to convert them into buying customers, our customers. "R.A.P means Respond and Aggressively Pursue."

• Respond- by being the first to greet them on the lot or at the door. If a question is asked get the answer immediately. If you say you'll call them back, take 10 minutes out of your day, keep your word and call them back. Stay in contact with your customer.

• Aggressively Pursue- means that if they are there at your store; try your best to sell them now. But if they must leave, get their 1st and last name, cell phone and email. If you can get an address that would be a bonus. The objective is to get them back into the store as quick as possible. We are going to go after them smooth but close them hard and rock them to sleep. We are going to be relentless with keeping the lines of communication open. You must engage your customer with information and open ended questions. Set the appointment. You will not give a price over the phone.   Instead attempt to set the appointment for today. Stay aggressive. Remember you do this every day, all year long, your customer probably only does this once every three or four years, maybe longer. So stay professional. If you R.A.P with every customer you'll make more sales, and you know what more sales turn into?

$$$$ $$$$ $$$$ $$$$ Goal Setting is very important. I want you to list 5 things that you want to accomplish within the next 5 years. #1 being the most important goal and list the time frame (a month, day, and year) you want to have your goal accomplished. Use this goal sheet as motivation for you to excel beyond greatness in your sales position.

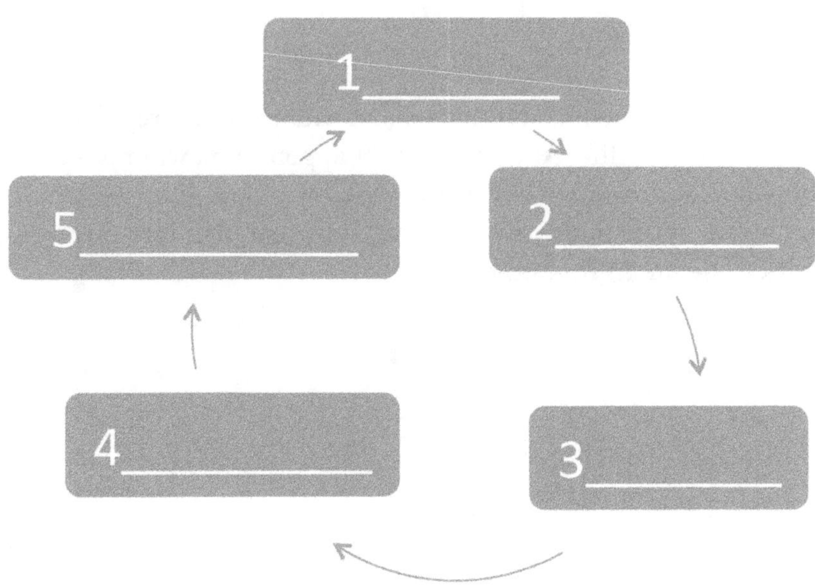

Maybe your goal is to plan that next big trip to London. Write it down, and set a date to take the trip and how you plan to pay for it.

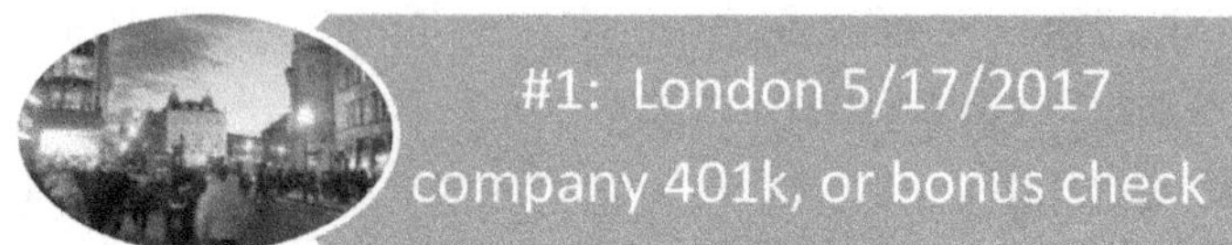

Example:

Once you get used to setting goals, it will become a regular routine in your life. And when that happens, you will notice how much more smoothly things will be in your life. Always set a goal, write it down, it's a plan. Turn that plan into rewards, perks, and smart investments.

The 10 Sale Commandments

1. Be Confident
2. Never lie to your customer
3. Never force your customer to lie to you. By asking them uncomfortable, personal questions- that will make them put up their defenses.
4. Build value by knowing what you are talking about. Product knowledge is crucial.
5. Stay in your seat and negotiate.
6. Close your own deals; take the credit application, politely ask for the money down, sell the paint and fabric protection, plant the seed for an extended warranty/ service contract
7. Pay attention to detail, be thorough.
8. Fill out all paperwork completely before it goes into Finance.
9. If you promise-deliver.
10. Follow up after the sale. Follow up one day, then one week, and then one month and then every 6 months after the sale. The goal here is to generate a referral/ lead. And if nothing else, you're letting the customer know that they're on your mind.

Generating leads

Other than lot traffic/foot traffic, which there doesn't seem to be very much of these days, what are other forms of effectively generating leads?

- Member of a business network incorporative (BNI member)
- Join your local Chamber of Commerce Group.
- Promoting a referral fee through your local churches, offer the pastor's a donation to the church for every member you sell. One big church or four small churches, visit each one each a month.
- Internet leads, such as through your dealership website, trucar.com, autotrader.com, cars.com, Edmonds.com, ford direct, gmauto.com, maybe even signing up through automart.com
- Purchase a customer lead sheet from a marketing firm and cold call.
- Craigslist ads
- YouTube commercial or advertisement
- Attend sorority and fraternity functions and network
- Your dealership's service log is a gold mine. Run a report and call them up.
- ____
- ____
- ____
- ____

Your main goal is to set the appointment and prepare for the sale. Below are some fire techniques that have been applied over the years to get results…

Script #1: Sales person: **"Hello, This is (your name) from (your dealership). I'm calling because your vehicle was in our service department yesterday. I was wondering with such a nice looking vehicle how come you're not taking advantage of the equity in your vehicle?"** Customer Response; {most likely will be one of or several listed below}

1. Customer talks about car problems 2."What equity?" 3. "How much Equity?" 4. "What is my car worth?" 5. "Who are you again?" 6. "Are you trying to sell me a new car?" 7. "My car is paid for." 8. "I can't afford a car note." 9. "How much money are you talking about?" 10. "How much do I have to put down?"

Sales person Response: **"I'd simply like to present you with some information. I called to set a time for us to meet, have a soda or coffee and give you some options for upgrading. If you don't like what I'm saying when you get here then we'll shake hands and part as friends. And I'll give you $10.00 for your gas. I have an opening on my calendar for 2:11p.m. today. (This technique will get your customer to remember their appointment because the time is unusual therefore leaves an impression) Do you have a piece of paper and a pen?" (Wait until the customer gets the paper and pen.)**

*****Give the customer your first and last name, your cell**

phone number and then confirm that you will see them today at 2:11p.m. or whatever time you agreed upon. Confirm that they have proper directions and confirm the time once more.

Script # 2: Sales Person: "Hi, I'm (your name) form (your dealership) I'm calling to set an appointment to meet with you, in regards to your vehicle."
Customer: "What about my car?"
Sales Person: "I noticed it was recently in our service department and I was curious about what's wrong with it?"
Customer: Explaining problems.
Sales Person: "Wow! Well I'd like to present you some options that will help. It's important we meet today, 3:35 is great for me or is later better for you?"
Customer: will set the time with you. Always bump the time up 3 minutes to stress the importance of this meeting.
Sales Person Close appointment: *Give the customer your first and last name, your cell phone number and then confirm that you will see them today at whatever time you agreed upon. Confirm that they have proper directions and confirm the time once more.*

The differences between script one and script two should be very obvious. Although obvious to the experienced ear, these methods and techniques are seldom if ever used. Both are very effective. **Script 1** gently leads the customers up to the appointment, while showing genuine concern through the use of charisma.

Script 2 is more direct and very engaging. It invites the customer to share information so that you can stress the importance of meeting you.

Lesson 4: Marketing and Advertising

Marketing & Advertising

Various forms of marketing and advertising must be done in order for any business or organization to make sales and consistently make a profit. Though there are exceptions to the rule, for the most part we cannot abandon our core methods of advertising. As old fashioned as they may seem, our core forms of advertising are an integral plan to tell the world of consumers that your business is here, it's the best product with the best customer service open for all to come and visit.

SO WHAT TYPES OF MARKETING ARE THERE?

1. Grass Roots / Word of mouth
   * Sales people & customers do all the talking (good and bad press)
   * Handing out flyers
   * Passing out business cards
   * Network with friends and family
   * Post card mailer
   * Ask previous customers for referrals

** This type of marking is traditional. It's very time consuming and can create a very slow grind for sales. But it's the most personable source of marketing to date.

2. Print Marketing
   * Newspaper
   * Magazines
   * Postal mail

- Book reviews
- Auto trader

** This type of advertising is very dated and also difficult to track your campaign dollars. Unless you advertise in a highly publicized magazine or print forum, you could be throwing your money in the wind. Print media is good if done in conjunction with some other form of advertisement.

3. Media Forums
   - AM/ FM Radio
   - XM/ Sirius Radio
   - Television

** This form of advertising is very useful for letting people know that your business exist. But in order for this type of advertising to be successful you must be seen or heard in constant rotation for at least 60 to 90 days. However, when advertising through media forums there aren't any methods for you to track or know who your customer base is. That's because media forums weren't designed for you to track your customer. Media forums were designed to simply tell the world that you are here, planting a seed by staying on the consumers mind.

4. Digital & Social Media/ Internet marketing
   - Craigslist
   - Face book
   - Cars.com
   - Edmonds.com
   - Twitter
   - Yahoo business
   - Google Reviews

- Auto trader.com
- Your company website
- Mass Email Blasts
- Amazon.com
- EBay

** This form of advertising is very effective in generating sales because you reach a broader target group and this method is cost effective for those who are on a tight budget. The internet brings the world a lot closer and if utilized correctly you can reap substantial profits.

There are no magical tricks to marketing or sales. There are no secret formulas, people buy from and where they feel comfortable and familiar. Therefore each form of marketing must be consistent with its message toward the target group or core groups that you are aiming for. Marketing also depends on the region in which you are targeting. Also consider the average household income of your target market. Is your target market a particular ethnic group or gender? What age group are you targeting? Find out what is important to people in your community and focus on that desire ("hot button") and you will be successful.

Helpful Sales Tips

-Suggestive selling is a skill that few people know that they have. Suggestive selling offers good choices and gives credit-ability to your character without seeming pushy.
-Simply inform them of their options that they may not be aware of, always be unique and get creative.
-Never rate your customer, attempt to read your customer or size them up. Instead engage your customer with opened ended questions so that they will interact with you, not follow you around.
-Always keep the conversation flowing, this keeps the customer engaged and enables you to use trial closes regarding the price, payment or benefit of features.
-Mannerisms, tone and inflection make the difference; always stay up beat and professional.
-Always Smile.

Log onto: www.trouthousepub.com
Look for more products and exciting authors from Trout House Publishing Group.

www.ingramcontent.com/pod-product-compliance
Lightning Source LLC
Chambersburg PA
CBHW071448030726
47593CB00003B/947